STUDIES IN ECONOM

Inflation and UK Monetary Policy

Third Edition

Mark Russell
Lord Wandsworth College

and

David F. Heathfield
Formerly University of Southampton

Series Editor
Susan Grant
West Oxfordshire College

Heinemann

To Ivor Pearce, teacher and friend

Heinemann Educational Publishers
Halley Court, Jordan Hill, Oxford OX2 8EJ
a division of Reed Educational & Professional Publishing Ltd

OXFORD MELBOURNE AUCKLAND
JOHANNESBURG BLANTYRE GABORONE
IBADAN PORTSMOUTH (NH) USA CHICAGO

Heinemann is a registered trademark of Reed Educational & Professional Publishing Ltd

© Mark Russell and David F. Heathfield, 1996, 1999
© David F. Heathfield, 1992 (1st edition)

First published as *UK inflation*, 1992, in the Studies in the UK Economy series.
Second edition published as *Inflation and UK monetary policy* in 1996, also in the Studies in the UK Economy series.
Third edition published 1999

03 02 01 00 99
10 9 8 7 6 5 4 3 2 1

All rights reserved.

Apart from any fair dealing for the purposes of research or private study, or criticism or review as permitted under the terms of the UK Copyright, Designs and Patents Act, 1988, this publication may not be reproduced, stored or transmitted, in any form or by any means, without the prior permission in writing of the publishers, or in the case of reprographic reproduction only in accordance with the terms of the licences issued by the Copyright Licensing Agency in the UK, or in accordance with the terms of licences issued by the appropriate Reproduction Rights Organization outside the UK. Enquiries concerning reproduction outside the terms stated here should be sent to the publishers at the address printed on this page.

British Library Cataloguing in Publication Data
A catalogue record for this book is available from the British Library

ISBN 0 435 33213 9

Typeset and illustrated by TechType, Abingdon, Oxon.
Printed and bound in Great Britain by Biddles Ltd, Guildford.

Acknowledgements

The publishers would like to thank the following for permission to reproduce copyright material: AEB for the questions on pp. 74, 99; The Bank of England for the material on pp. 18, 42, 44, 56, 80, 90, 95, 99–100; The *Economist* for the cartoon and extract on p. 23; The Edexcel Foundation for the questions on pp. 20–1, 110; The *Financial Times* for the figure on p. 103; The *Guardian* for the article 'For Euro-lovers only the language is new', (7 June 1991), on pp. 121–2; HMSO for the material on p. 21; Crown copyright is reproduced with the permission of Her Majesty's Stationery Office; The *Independent* for the article 'Interview: Milton Friedman', by John Lichfield, *Independent on Sunday*, 26/7/92, on p. 35; National Institute Economic Review for the material on pp. 59, 85; OCR for the questions on pp. 29–30, 47, 59, 74–5, 85, 99–100, 110, 121–2; The Office for National Statistics for the material on pp. 56, 75,111; The *Telegraph* for the cartoon by Matt on p. 97.

The publishers have made every effort to contact copyright holders. However, if any material has been incorrectly acknowledged, the publishers would be pleased to correct this at the earliest opportunity.

Contents

Preface and acknowledgements .... *iv*

Introduction *1*

Chapter One — Defining inflation *3*

Chapter Two — Measuring inflation *11*

Chapter Three — Costs and benefits of inflation *22*

Chapter Four — Conflicting views on the causes of inflation *31*

Chapter Five — Inflation in the UK *49*

Chapter Six — The basis of monetary policy *60*

Chapter Seven — Implementing monetary policy *76*

Chapter Eight — Current UK monetary policy *86*

Chapter Nine — The wider impact of monetary policy *101*

Chapter Ten — European economic and monetary union *112*

Conclusion *122*

Index *123*

Preface

This is the third edition of a popular title. Since the publication of the second edition there have been new A level specifications, changes in the UK's experience of inflation, and in UK monetary policy. This edition addresses those changes.

The book tackles a difficult area in a lucid manner. It covers the key areas of inflation and acknowledges differences of opinion about the causes and consequences of inflation. The now firm link between inflation and monetary policy is stressed, and – after reviewing past UK monetary policy – the authors focus on the nature and effects of current monetary policy.

Students and teachers will welcome particularly the interesting and well-informed coverage of the role of the monetary policy committee provided in Chapter 8.

Susan Grant
Series Editor

Acknowledgements

This book has benefited greatly from the observations and guidance of Sue Grant. A number of present and former students have assisted us on this and previous editions in making the book a more readable and accurate volume by their comments. For this third edition we are grateful to George Bayer for comments on the entire manuscript, and Mads Dal, Katy Pelling and Edward Walker for comments on individual chapters. Any remaining errors are, of course, our own.

MCR and DFH
May 1999

Introduction

The area of inflation, a relatively new phenomenon in an historical context, is now well known and understood. How best to measure it and what causes it are still areas of dispute, however. Monetary policy is an ever-changing beast. Even as this book is being written there is a great deal of doubt about what the future holds – and indeed if the UK will even have its own monetary policy in a few years time.

Inflation and monetary policy matter to everyone. Inflation affects the ability of households and firms to make sensible decisions. The consequences of inflation can be significant to the well-being of the whole economy. The implementation of monetary policy, with its effect on interest rates, directly impacts on households and firms as the cost of borrowing and saving changes.

This book can be divided into two. In the first part we examine inflation itself; in the second part we examine the policy to deal with inflation.

In Chapter 1 we explain inflation and in Chapter 2 how it is measured. Chapter 3 examines the potential costs and benefits of inflation, and Chapter 4 what might cause inflation. In Chapter 5 we examine how inflation has behaved in the UK.

The theoretical basis of monetary policy, why and how it should work is the subject of Chapter 6. In Chapter 7 we look at the various ways in which monetary policy has been applied since the 1970s. In Chapter 8 the current arrangements for monetary policy are examined. This is a very new area for most of us – exactly how monetary policy is organized, and what its objectives are, are far from clear to those who read the national press. If your interest is only in how monetary policy is conducted at present then you should be able to read Chapter 8 on its own.

Chapter 9 explains the wider impact of monetary policy on the economy. All decisions on monetary policy affect the everyday lives of households and firms. Students of Business Studies will find this chapter of use in understanding why business organizations are so concerned with interest rate decisions.

Finally, in Chapter 10, we look at European monetary union, and its implications for UK monetary policy whether the UK joins or not.

In line with the new syllabus and specifcation requirements, the book uses aggregate demand and aggregate supply analysis rather than the more traditional Keynesian income/expenditure approach. For those unfamiliar with this analysis, suggested further reading references are provided at the end of each chapter.

The book is designed to cover the needs of those taking either the current A level syllabuses or the new A level specifications to be introduced in September 2000. Indeed we have made a point of meeting all requirements of the new specifications. The increased length of the third edition has also allowed us to provide sufficient coverage for students taking introductory courses in economics and business at a university.

Chapter One

Defining inflation

'*Inflation means that your money won't buy as much today as it did when you didn't have any.*'
Anonymous

What is being inflated?

It is difficult to trace the time when the word '**inflation**' began to take on its modern meaning. Inflation today is taken to mean a *sustained rise in the aggregate, or general, price level*. The experience of the 1970s, when inflation reached levels not previously experienced in the UK, meant that control of inflation became the main aim of the UK government policy since the 1980s. It has become a widely held view that a stable price level is a necessary precondition for the reduction of unemployment and the promotion of economic growth. As Nigel Lawson, Chancellor of the Exchequer from 1983 to 1989, put it:

'*We set as the overriding objective of macroeconomic policy the conquest of inflation.*'

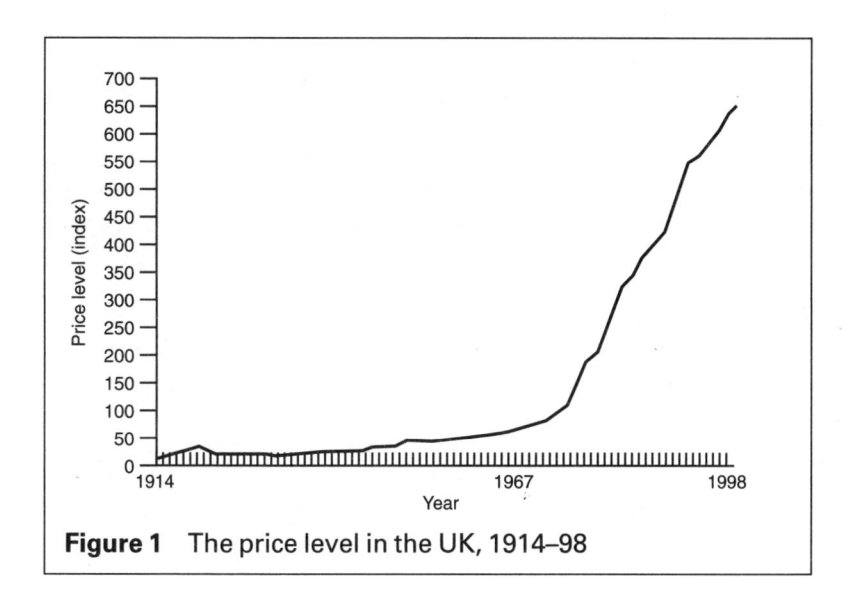

Figure 1 The price level in the UK, 1914–98

Inflation and UK Monetary Policy

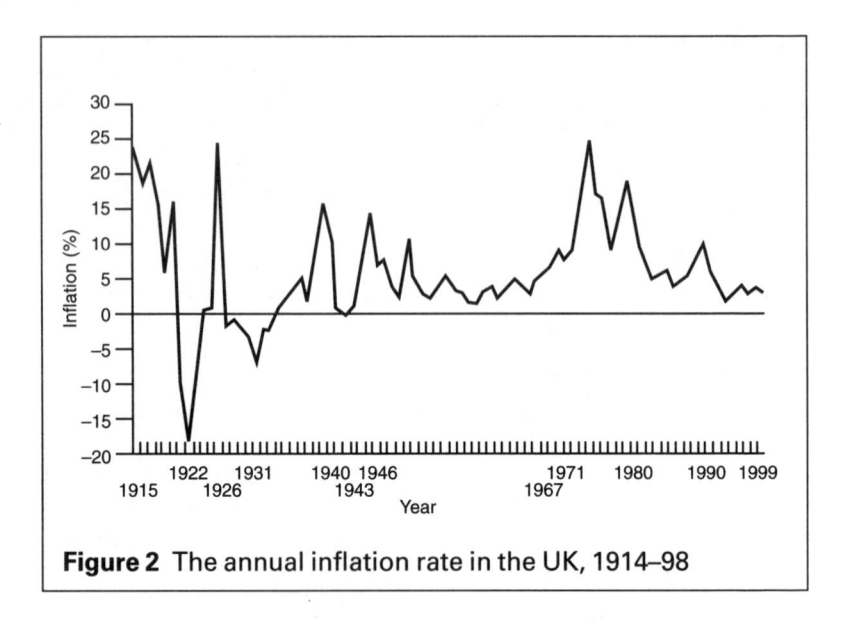

Figure 2 The annual inflation rate in the UK, 1914–98

Low inflation has not always been given the highest priority in economic policy. As Figure 1 shows, the **price level** in the UK has risen much more rapidly since 1945 – and especially since 1967 – than earlier in the century. This change has shaped modern opinions about inflation.

Figure 2 shows the annual rate of inflation since 1915. This demonstrates more clearly than Figure 1 the variability of the rate of inflation. Indeed, **deflation** occurred in many years – that is a fall in the aggregate price level. The overall effect of inflation and deflation meant that in 1914 the price level in the UK was about the same as in 1815, the end of the Napoleonic wars. Since 1945 there has been only one year when inflation did not occur, and so inflation is a modern phenomenon and one that needs to be explained.

The price mechanism

One of the major contributions made by economists, for a greater understanding of how our society works, is the analysis of the price mechanism. Largely as a result of the work of Adam Smith, we have come to see that if individual economic agents – workers, landowners, shoppers, investors etc. – buy at the lowest prices and sell at the highest prices, then both they as individuals, and society as a whole, will be as well off as it is possible to be (in a material sense).

Defining inflation

When there are shortages, sellers raise prices, and this encourages suppliers to supply more and encourages buyers to look for alternative goods. When there are surpluses, prices fall, which discourages suppliers and encourages buyers. Figure 3 shows the effects on prices and quantities of:

- an increase in demand from D_1 to D_2 with no change in the position of the supply curve
- an increase in supply from S_1 to S_2 with no change in the position of the demand curve.

What this demonstrates is that flexible prices are necessary for markets to work efficiently. Price fluctuations will signal to suppliers and to consumers where there are shortages and where there are surpluses, and suppliers will adjust output in response to these signals.

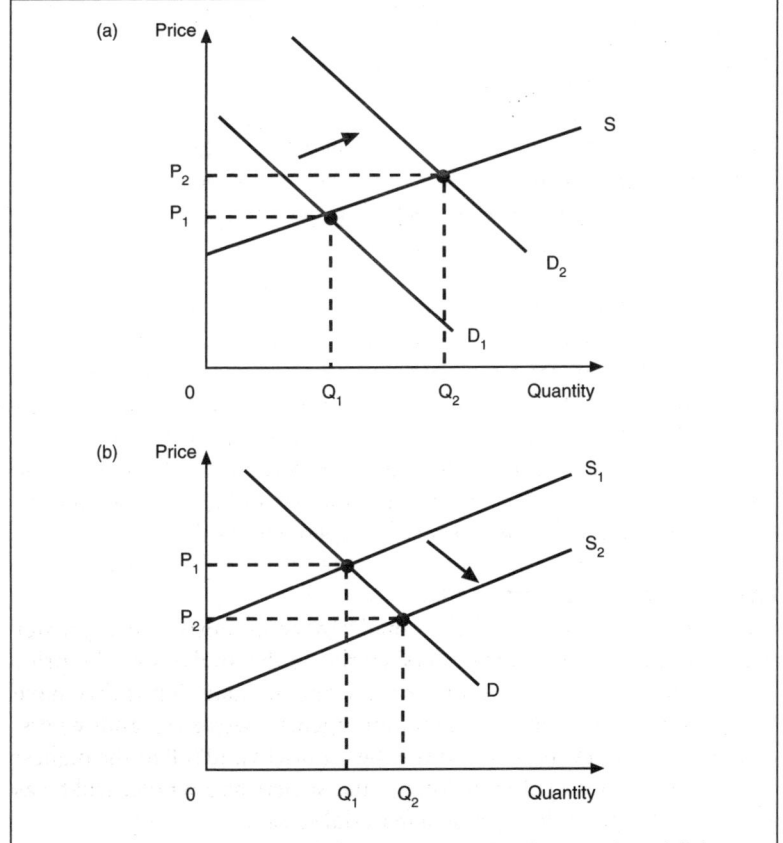

Figure 3 The effects of (a) an increase in demand and (b) an increase in supply

In a dynamic, ever-changing, free-market economy we would expect prices to be always on the move – some going up and some going down and perhaps a few remaining the same. For example, the price of fresh flowers on Mothering Sunday is two or three times higher than on the following day. All year, supermarkets cover their windows with information about price reductions and invite us to buy 'while prices are low'.

The price mechanism works by causing resources to be allocated to the production of certain goods. A change in the *relative* prices of two goods, say bread and potatoes, is enough to cause consumers to buy more of one and less of the other. Firms, in this case farmers, will alter the mix of products they produce in response to this price change.

The question that concerns us is – what is happening to prices *on average*? Relative prices must, and do, change but relative prices are not our concern. We are here concerned only with their aggregate (average) behaviour.

Purchasing power

Many commentators believe that in the best of all possible worlds there would be no change in the general level of prices. Relative prices would be adjusted in such a way that each price rise would be exactly balanced by a price fall elsewhere. Achieving this exactly is unlikely. The average price level will fluctuate, but if these fluctuations even out over time there is no long-run tendency for the general level of price to rise or fall. What almost everyone wants to avoid is a sustained rise in the general level of prices.

To see what inflation means for those on fixed incomes, consider households with £100 to spend every week. They have to decide each week which are the best buys to put in their shopping baskets. As relative prices change, the best buys change too, so goods whose prices have fallen are substituted for those whose prices have risen; but, on balance, with no inflation, the shoppers are as well off every week.

If, however, there is inflation (i.e. price rises are not compensated for by price falls elsewhere) then the shoppers become progressively worse off. As time goes by the £100 buys fewer goods.

This gives us another way of defining inflation – it is the *secular decline in the purchasing power of money*. With each successive year the pound is worth less in terms of the goods it can buy, and so inflation can be seen as a secular erosion of the value of the currency.

Table 1 shows how the value of the pound sterling – in terms of its ability to be exchanged for goods in the UK – has changed between 1920 and 1998.

Table 1 Purchasing power of the pound (1920 = 100)

1920	1925	1930	1935	1940	1945	1950	1955
100	125	135	157	129	111	98	76

1960	1965	1970	1975	1980	1985	1990	1995	1998
66	56	46	27	13	8.9	6.8	5.8	5.33

Reading along the rows, we see that £100 in 1920 would buy fewer goods than in 1935, when you could buy half as much again for your £100 – i.e. £157-worth of 1920 goods. Average price level had therefore been falling over that period. Since 1935, however, the pound has lost value. By 1950, £100 would buy the same amount of goods as in 1920, and by 1998, £100 would buy only the same amount of goods as £5.33 would buy in 1920. Someone who put his savings under his mattress in 1920 would have lost almost 95 per cent of the value 78 years later!

Pure inflation

Of course, inflation can occur even when there are no changes in relative prices. If the price of every good were to double, then *relative* prices would remain unchanged but the *aggregate* price level would double. The shopper would find that £100 would buy only half the quantity of goods and there would be no price incentive to switch from some goods to others. Inflation of this kind – let us call it **pure inflation** – has no role to play in the efficient operation of the price mechanism since there are no changes in relative prices to reflect relative shortages (or surpluses).

This leads us to the distinction between real values and nominal values. The **real** value of money is given by the goods and services it can buy. The real value of £100 halved when the price level doubled, while the **nominal**, or money value, of the £100 remains the same. To allow a clearer picture of how relative prices have changed it is common to report statistics in **real terms**; that is, the nominal value is adjusted to take account of the effects of inflation. In Chapter 2 we show how this adjustment is made.

The rate of inflation

Until now we have considered increases in price level but have said nothing about how long it takes for these changes to come about. In what follows we shall be considering the rate of change of price level –

the **rate of inflation**. Typically we shall be comparing the price level at one point in time with the price level one year later. This is what is meant by the year-on-year figure and it measures the annual rate of inflation for a particular twelve-month period.

If price level doubled in one year then the annual rate of inflation would be 100 per cent, but if this doubling of price level took 35 years then the annual rate of inflation would be only 2 per cent. It is the rate of change of price level which is of interest rather than the absolute change in price level. Few shoppers would be too concerned at an annual rate of inflation of only 2 per cent but many would look askance at 100 per cent in a year.

Degrees of inflation

It has been suggested that four degrees of inflation can be helpfully, if somewhat arbitrarily, distinguished.

- First there is **creeping inflation** which is persistent but at a low level – less than 10 per cent.
- Second comes **severe inflation** which occurs at rates between 10 and 100 per cent.
- Third is **galloping inflation,** at between 100 and 1000 per cent.
- Finally there is **hyperinflation** (greater than 1000 per cent a year) which gets so high as to lead to the destruction of the currency.

Hyperinflation

When there is hyperinflation the currency can be used neither as a medium of exchange nor as a store of value. The rate at which money is losing its purchasing power is so rapid that between someone receiving wages and spending them they will have lost an appreciable amount of their value. No-one therefore wants to hold or use money. This applies equally to those who are selling and those who are buying. Shopkeepers are reluctant to sell (exchange their goods for money) when the value of the money is falling all the time. They have no confidence that the money they accept will purchase as many goods and services for them as they have exchanged for it.

After the First World War hyperinflations occurred in Austria, Germany, Hungary, Poland and Russia. In Germany the price level rose by 100 *billion* per cent.

After the Second World War, hyperinflations affected China, Greece and Hungary. The worst case was that of Hungary where inflation reached its peak of 42 000 *thousand billion* per cent in July 1946. This resulted in an increase in price level in Hungary of 3.8 per cent with 27 noughts on the end. Russia suffered hyperinflation between 1990 and 1994 as chaos followed the collapse of the communist regime.

It is the experience of hyperinflation and its destruction of currencies – particularly in Europe in the first half of this century – which lies at the root of many people's terror of inflation. To them, inflation of any kind will tend to lead to hyperinflation and hyperinflation must be avoided at all costs. We look at this again later.

Summing up
In the UK and in most developed countries it is clear that:
- There have been fluctuations in the rate of inflation, but almost all changes are positive so that the price level continues to rise – albeit at an uneven rate.
- All countries have experienced inflation.
- There is a very wide variation in rates of inflation among countries.

The phenomenon of inflation is therefore widespread, uneven, feared and in need of explanation.

KEY WORDS

Inflation	Nominal
Price level	Real terms
Deflation	Rate of inflation
Price mechanism	Creeping inflation
Pure inflation	Severe inflation
Real	Galloping inflation

Further reading
CSO, *Retail Price Index Business Monitor MM23*, HMSO.
EBEA, Unit 11 in *Core Economics*, Heinemann Educational, 1995.
Heathfield, D. and Russell, M., Chapter 16 in *Modern Economics*, 2nd edn, Harvester Wheatsheaf, 1992.
Wilkinson, M., Chapters 1 and 2 in *Equity, Efficiency and Market Failure*, Heinemann Educational, 1997.

Chapter Two
Measuring inflation

'There are lies, damned lies and statistics.'
Disraeli

To measure the annual rate of change of the price of a good we have to measure the price at one point in time and measure it again 12 months later. A kilo of sugar, for example, may sell for £1.50 on 1 January 2000 and for £2.00 on 1 January 2001. The increase in price is therefore easily measured as 50p over the 12-month period. The annual rate of change of the price of sugar will then be given by change of price divided by the original price: 0.5/1.5 = 0.3333, or about 33 per cent.

If the prices of all goods rose at the same rate then measuring inflation would be easy. Unfortunately there is rarely, if ever, an occurrence of such pure inflation. Typically some prices rise a lot, others rise only a little, some remain unchanged and others fall. The problem then is to measure the 'aggregate' price when there is no common behaviour among individual prices.

There is no ideal solution to this question but there are plenty of second-best solutions.

Retail price index

In 1947 the **retail price index** (RPI) became the basic measure of domestic inflation in the UK. The aim of the RPI is to measure how the purchasing power of ordinary consumers is being affected by rising prices, the prices that affect consumers (final users of the goods and services) being the prices 'in the shops', retail prices.

In order to compute this price index the government set out to discover the expenditure pattern of a typical UK household via a large-scale *Household Expenditure Survey*. A sample of households throughout the UK were asked to report on how they spent their incomes, and from this information a typical **'basket' of goods** is constructed representing the average purchases made. Changes in the cost of this basket are used to calculate the RPI. Since 1957 there has been an annual survey of some 7000 households (the *Family Expenditure Survey* or FES), and these surveys provide the basis for the basket underlying the RPI. These 7000 households exclude both pensioner households (where three-quarters of income comes from pensions) and the top 4 per cent of households by income.

The expenditure pattern is, of course, changing all the time. We no longer rely on candles to light our houses and offices, and rarely burn coal to heat them. We do, however, buy video recorders and compact discs which simply were not available when the index was started. The appropriate basket is therefore continually changing and we are faced with the problem of deciding what our basket should contain.

The solution is to keep the basket fixed for a year at a time but to revise the basket every year in line with changes in the pattern of expenditure. Thus the FES has to be carried out every year.

The RPI in 1998

The basket for 1998 comprised some 600 separate indicators and is shown in Figure 4. It is clear that our greatest expenditure is on housing and household goods, and this is followed by travel and leisure and then by food and catering.

If our total expenditure – the whole basket – is given the value of 1000 points, then expenditure on housing and household goods would constitute 359 points, travel and leisure would be 263 points, food and catering 178 points, alcohol and tobacco 105 points and personal expenditure 105 points. These 'points' represent the relative importance of these items in consumers' expenditure and are called **weights**. The areas devoted to each item in the pie-chart reflect these weights, so that 'housing and household expenditure' is about three and a half times as big as 'personal expenditure'. The larger the weight the bigger the influence it has on the RPI. Thus if the price of 'housing and household expenditure' (359 points) rose by 10 per cent it would have three and a half times the effect on the RPI as would a 10 per cent rise in the price of 'personal expenditure' (105 points).

Now we have the basket for 1998 we need information on the price changes of each of its elements. The RPI is intended to be a measure of how much aggregate price level has *changed* rather than a measure of the level of aggregate prices. Every month 150 000 price movements of some 600 types of goods and services in 180 towns and cities are monitored and combined into a single figure using the weights of the basket.

The RPI therefore measures the monthly change in the value of a basket of consumer goods. The basket represents the expenditure pattern of a typical household and is updated every year to reflect the changing expenditure patterns over time.

These month-on-month changes can be linked together to provide comparisons of aggregate price levels between years. Figure 5 shows how the RPI has behaved between 1971 and 1998. It will be evident from this figure that inflation – the rate of change of aggregate price

Inflation and UK Monetary Policy

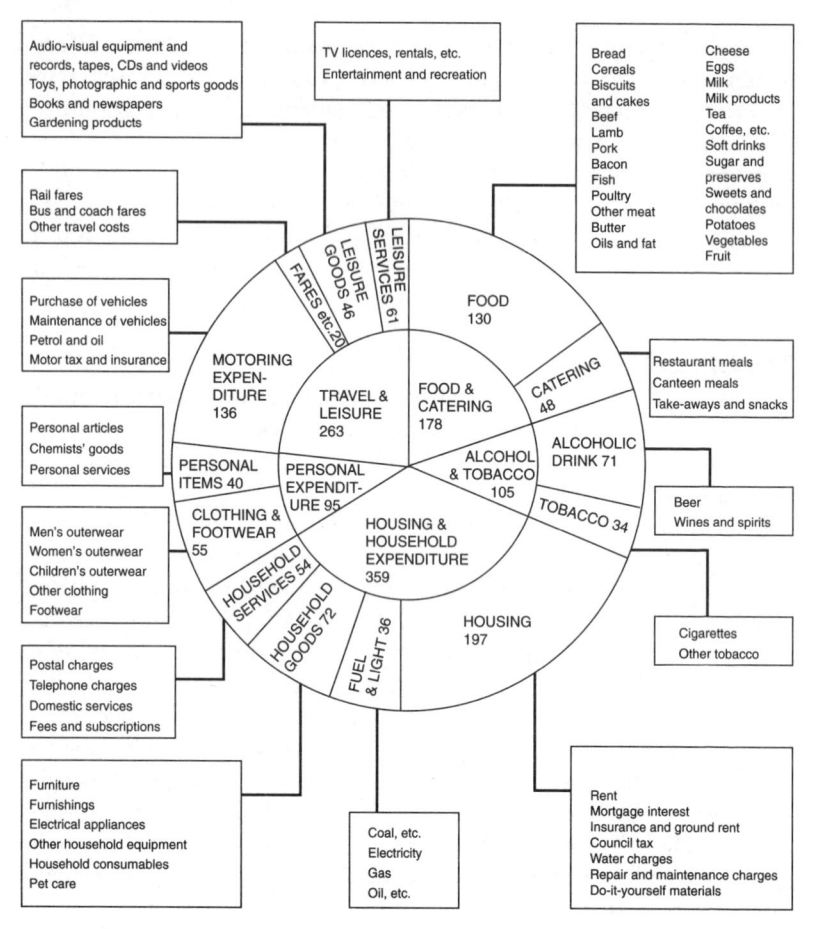

Figure 4 The structure of the RPI in 1998

level – has varied quite a lot, with the highest rate being over 25 per cent a year and the lowest being less than 2 per cent a year. The aggregate price level never fell (or even remained constant) during those 27 years.

Constructing the RPI

As its name suggests the RPI is an index, and uses index numbers to express the price level rather than some average price. In the first year of the index – the base year – the index is set at 100. If prices rise by 10 per cent in the first year the index rises to 110. If prices rise by 10 per cent in the second year the *index* rises another 10 per cent, to 121 (*not* 10 points).

Measuring inflation

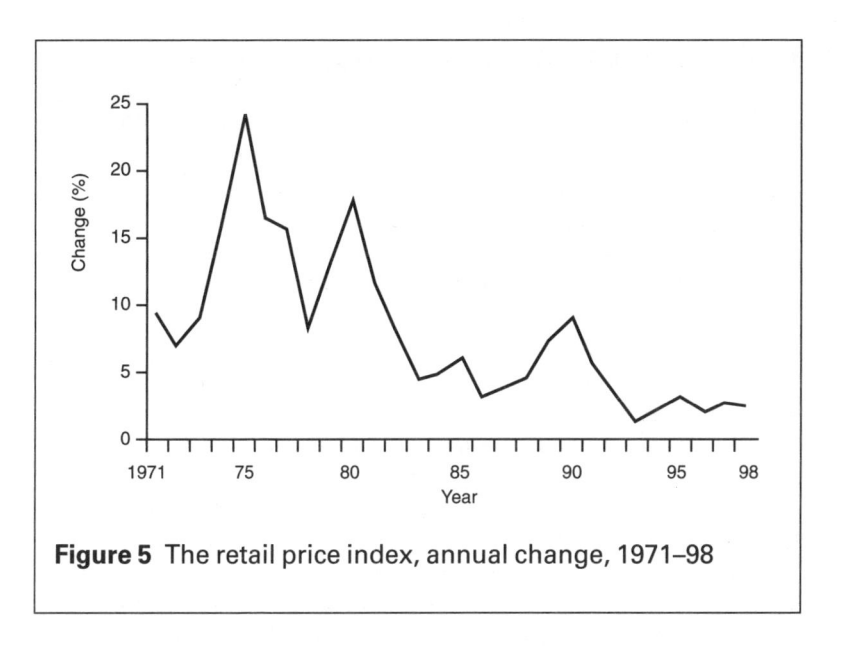

Figure 5 The retail price index, annual change, 1971–98

The monthly figures for 1994 and early 1995 in Table 2 show that the price index rose from 100 in January to 102.41 in May and June, when it reached a short plateau before rising again fairly steadily upwards. These monthly figures allow us to compute the year-on-year inflation rate. For example, from February 1994 to February 1995 the index changed by 3.39 points, or about 3.37 per cent. The index for any month can be compared with that of the same month a year later to give the year-on-year, or annual, rate of inflation.

Table 2 Change in the retail price index from January 1994 (=100) to February 1995

Jan	Feb	Mar	Apr	May	Jun
100.00	100.57	100.85	102.05	102.41	102.41
Jul	Aug	Sep	Oct	Nov	Dec
101.91	102.41	102.62	102.76	102.83	103.33
Jan	Feb				
103.33	103.96				

Sources: *Monthly Digest of Statistics* (various) and *Retail Price Index* (MM23), February 1994.

Table 3 Example of a representative basket of goods

	Quantity	1999 price	2000 price	1999 value	2000 value	Change in value	Change in price (%)
Bread	4 kilo	£0.50	£1.00	£2.00	£4.00	+£2.00	+100
Tea	2 kilo	£2.50	£2.00	£5.00	£4.00	-£1.00	-20
Cloth	1 metre	£5.00	£5.00	£5.00	£5.00	£0.00	0
Coal	4 kilo	£2.00	£3.00	£8.00	£12.00	+£4.00	+50
Totals				£20.00	£25.00	+£5.00	

- **A representative basket – an example**

Consider for the moment a rather simple economy in which there are only four goods – say bread, tea, cloth and coal. Each has its price in pounds so that, for example in 1999, bread costs £0.50 per kilo, tea £2.50 per kilo, cloth £5.00 per square metre and coal £2.00 per kilo. Twelve months later, in 2000, the price of bread has increased by 100 per cent to £1.00 per kilo, that of tea has fallen by 20 per cent to £2.00 per kilo, that of cloth has remained unchanged and that of coal has risen by 50 per cent to £3.00 per kilo.

Relative prices have clearly changed and there is no single good which can be taken as representative of goods in general. It is therefore necessary to construct a representative basket of goods.

To see how this works, suppose a survey finds that the average combination (basket) of goods purchased comprises four kilos of bread, two kilos of tea, one square metre of cloth and four kilos of coal. To buy this basket of goods at their original prices would cost £20.00, which is therefore the 'price' of the basket. In 2000 that same basket of goods would cost £25.00. The aggregate price – the price of the basket of goods – has therefore risen by £5.00, or 25 per cent of the original.

The choice of basket is crucial, as it is possible to change the measured rate of inflation by altering the content of the basket. For example, if more tea were added to the basket the measured rate of inflation would be less because the price of tea fell during the period.

There are two ways of measuring inflation with this basket of goods. The first is simply to use the formula:

$$\text{Price index} = \frac{\text{Cost of basket now}}{\text{Cost of basket in base year}} \times 100$$

The **base year** is the year in which you wish to start your index and will equal 100 (note that there are no units attached). For example, our base year is 1999 and we can see that applying the formula gives an index number of 100:

$$\text{Price index} = \frac{\text{Cost of basket in 1999}}{\text{Cost of basket in base year}} \times 100$$

$$= \frac{£20}{£20} \times 100 = 100.$$

For 2000 we find that the index has risen to 125:

$$\text{Price index} = \frac{\text{Cost of basket in 2000}}{\text{Cost of basket in base year}} \times 100$$

$$= \frac{£25}{£20} \times 100 = 125.$$

As 2000 is only the second year of the index it can easily be seen that the index has risen by 25 per cent and we can say that inflation was 25 per cent over the 12-month period. In subsequent years the rate of inflation is not quite so obvious. Suppose that in 2001 the index had risen to 137.5. The rise in the index is 12.5 and dividing 12.5 by 125 and multiplying by 100 tells us that the index has risen by 10 per cent.

The above method is simple, but difficult to use when constructing a large index. Instead we could give each good an index of its own and a weight according to its importance in the basket:

Good	Weight	Index in 1999
Bread	10% or 0.10	100
Tea	25% or 0.25	100
Cloth	25% or 0.25	100
Coal	40% or 0.40	100
Total	100% or 1.0	100

The weights are assigned according to the proportion of total expenditure each good accounts for in the basket in 1999. To find the index for 1999 each goods' index is multiplied by its weight and the four resulting totals are added up:

Good	Weight		Index in 1999		
Bread	0.10	×	100	=	10
Tea	0.25	×	100	=	25
Cloth	0.25	×	100	=	25
Coal	0.40	×	100	=	40
Total	1.00				100

We can see that the index in 1999 is 100. If we now apply the price changes for 1999 to the index for each good we find that the overall index has risen to 125:

Good	Weight		Index in 2000		
Bread	0.10	×	200	=	20
Tea	0.25	×	80	=	20
Cloth	0.25	×	100	=	25
Coal	0.40	×	150	=	60
Total	1.00				125

The RPI works by giving each class of good an index number and a weight out of 1000 as shown earlier. The RPI is then constructed as above. The advantage of this method is that it is possible to construct indexes (or indices) for groups of goods, such as catering or motoring.

Is the RPI accurate enough?

The RPI is often used to justify demands for higher money wages. If inflation measured by the RPI is 4 per cent, wage negotiations often ask for compensation. State pensions and benefits rise each year, but by how much need they rise to maintain the real value of the benefits?

- Average households?

The RPI does not reflect the true change in the purchasing power of most household incomes. We have seen that pensioner households are excluded from the Family Expenditure Survey and so the RPI 'basket' is influenced only by younger consumers. Pensioners often buy a different set of goods from working households, especially when considering housing costs – pensioners usually have no, or a very small, mortgage. When the rate of interest rises the RPI rises (in 1998 just under a fifth of the RPI basket was housing expenditure), but a pensioner with no mortgage and some savings is probably better off. By contrast, in 1998 nearly 30 per cent of pensioners' expenditure went on food, compared with the 13 per cent weight given to food in the RPI. Thus the RPI need not reflect the effect of changing prices of all groups or individuals accurately – it is only an average.

- Changes in quality

The RPI cannot distinguish between price rises that are due to inflation and those due to improved quality. Take a television set for example. A new colour television set in 1975 had far fewer features than one in 1999, so the quality of the good has improved. This implies more inputs into the product and the price has risen. While the RPI reads this as simple inflation, households are actually receiving more scarce resources for their money. Thus the RPI will overstate inflation whenever there are improvements in the quality of goods and services.

- **One-off shocks**

Recall that inflation is defined as the sustained rise in the general price level. This has led some commentators to argue that the effects of changing council tax rates and interest rates should be excluded from the index since they are once-and-for-all effects which distort the real (secular) inflation rate.

This desire to exclude certain items from the index extends much further than excluding council tax rates and interest rates. Some economists argue that the retail price index will be erroneous because it reflects changes in VAT and other indirect taxes. These are determined by the government and will be sharply changed from time to time according to circumstances and policies. Rarely will there be a persistant rise in any of these prices, and hence their influence on the retail price index should be excluded from any measure of the 'sustained rise in the general price level'.

Other consumer price indexes

An index that excludes mortgage interest rate, and another that also excludes local council taxes and indirect taxes, are published. Since these are supposed to truly reflect the inflation rate they are called the core inflation rates or the **underlying inflation** rates. To save any possible confusion, the full retail price index is referred to as **headline inflation**. The following is a summary of various published measures of inflation:

- RPI is the retail price index based on the basket of goods.
- TPI is RPI adjusted for changes in direct taxation (e.g. income tax).
- RPIX is the RPI less mortgage interest payments.
- RPIY is the RPIX less indirect taxes and duties (e.g. petrol duty and VAT).

The RPIX and RPIY are the 'underlying rates' referred to above, and Figure 6 shows how the RPIX and RPIY differ from the wider RPI definition.

The RPIX, the so-called underlying rate of inflation, is the one used by the Treasury to set the **'inflation target'** for the purposes of economic policy. This is because anti-inflation policy changes interest rates and these affect mortgage payments which have a weight of 45/1000 in the RPI (that is the same as all leisure goods combined). The RPIX therefore does not react directly to policy changes as the RPI does.

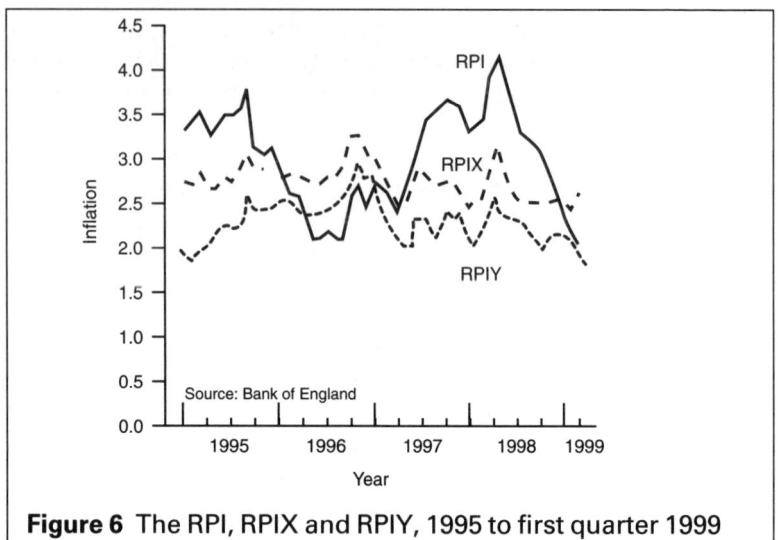

Figure 6 The RPI, RPIX and RPIY, 1995 to first quarter 1999

Other index measures

In addition to the RPI and the TPI there is a case for measuring inflation according to the price level faced by those who produce and sell UK goods and services – i.e. the factory-gate price index.

There are two major differences between the RPI and the factory-gate price index. First, the combination of goods produced in the UK differs from the combination bought by consumers in the UK. Some goods are produced in the UK but exported to foreigners and would be excluded from the RPI, while other goods are produced in the UK but bought by UK industry, for example machines. Some goods consumed by UK consumers are imported from abroad and so are not affected by changes in UK producer prices.

Second, the factory-gate price index would use different prices. The prices received by producers differ from the prices paid by consumers by the various taxes imposed between the factory gate and the shop counter (e.g. VAT).

The price index constructed using factory-gate prices and production quantities is called the **wholesale price index** or the 'index of producer prices'.

The choice of inflation index depends on which gives the best account of our economic performance. The RPI clearly is a good indicator of how inflation is affecting consumers, but the producers' output price index is the best indicator of UK production costs and

Measuring inflation

hence of our competitiveness in international markets. Finally, the producers' input price index provides an early indication of increases in producers' output prices.

Another type of price index is used, particularly in the construction of national accounts. These are known as 'price deflators' and relate to the whole economy. The Office for National Statistics (ONS) measures consumers' expenditure (*in toto*) both in current prices and in constant prices (e.g. at current prices and 1980 prices). Thus by dividing the current-priced value by the constant-priced value we can get a measure of the change in the aggregate price level. This measure is called the **consumers' expenditure deflator**. It is the index by which consumers' expenditure at current prices has to be 'deflated' to arrive at consumers' expenditure at constant prices. It will differ from the RPI insofar as it includes all the expenditure by households rather than that of a 'typical' household. Thus the expenditures by the very rich and the very poor are included.

The **GDP deflator** is constructed in the same way, but includes the prices of *all* goods produced within the UK and excludes the prices of imported goods. It is this index which is used to adjust UK national income statistics to *real* terms.

Recently the move towards closer integration of economies within the European Union has led to the construction of a measure of inflation that can be compared across all EU countries. This is known as the 'harmonized index of consumer prices' (HICP) and is discussed in Chapter 10.

As can be imagined there is much political interest in the construction and composition of these index numbers, and political parties tend to quote headline or core (underlying) inflation measures depending on which best supports their view of the world.

KEY WORDS

Retail price index	Inflation target
Basket of goods	Wholesale price index
Weights	Consumers' expenditure
Base year	deflator
Underlying inflation	GDP deflator
Headline inflation	

Further reading
Economic Review: Data Supplement (annual).
Griffiths, A. and Wall, S. (eds), Chapter 19 in *Applied Economics*, 7th edn, Addison-Wesley Longman, 1997.
Heathfield, D. and Russell, M., Chapter 12 in *Modern Economics*, 2nd edn., Harvester Wheatsheaf, 1992.
RPI Technical Manual, HMSO, 1998.

Useful website
ONS: www.ons.gov.uk/

Essay questions
1. (a) Explain what is meant by a weighted price index. [10 marks]
   (b) Discuss how accurate the RPI is as a measure of changes in the cost of living. [15 marks]
2. (a) Distinguish between the headline rate and the underlying rate of inflation. [10 marks]
   (b) Discuss the effects of inflation on the purchasing power of money and the clarity of signals sent through the price mechanism. [15 marks]

Data response question
This task is based on a question set by the University of London Examinations and Assessment Coucil in 1997. Figure A shows the weights used in compiling the retail price index (RPI) in 1995. Figures B and C show how spending patterns differ for housholds with different income levels. Study all the diagrams and then answer the following questions.

1. Explain how the weights in Figure B are determined. [3 marks]
2. With reference to Figure B, how might the weights for *two* of the following categories of spending have changed in their relative importance over the period since 1986: (i) tobacco; (ii) clothing; (iii) fuel and light? Justify your answers. [6 marks]
3. How would you account for the different proportions of household expenditure on (i) food and (ii) leisure goods and services, for households with different levels of income, as depicted in Figure A ? [4 marks]

Measuring inflation

Figure A Household expenditure on (a) food, and (b) leisure goods and services, by income group (percentages)

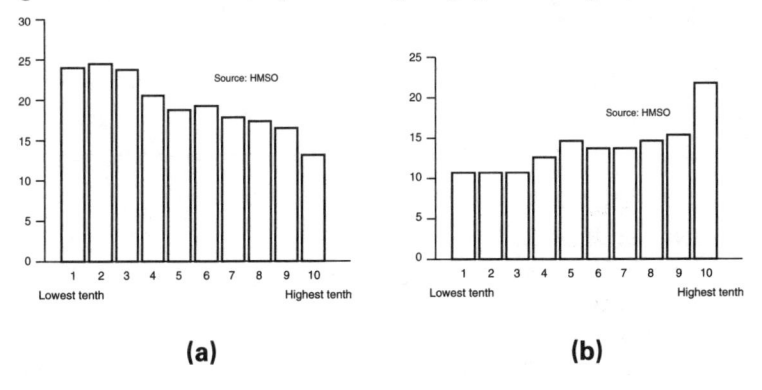

(a)

(b)

Figure B Weights used in compiling the retail price index in 1995 (total = 100)

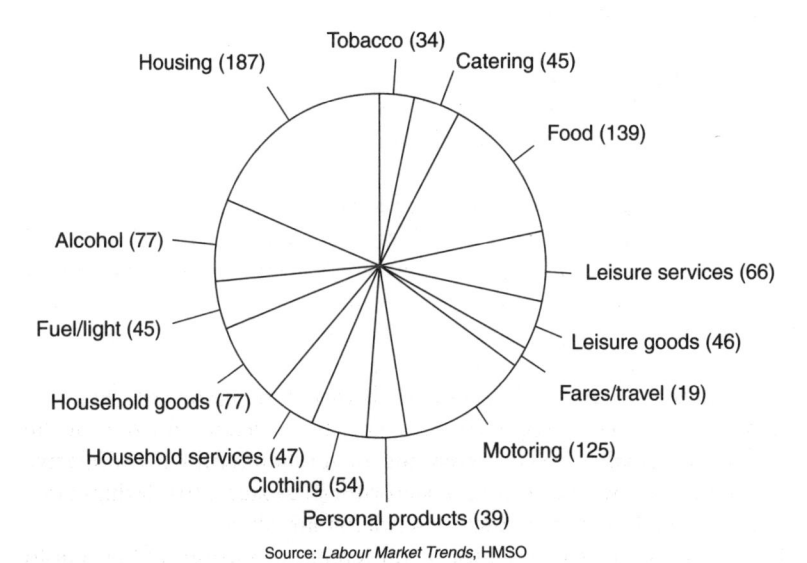

- Housing (187)
- Tobacco (34)
- Catering (45)
- Food (139)
- Leisure services (66)
- Leisure goods (46)
- Fares/travel (19)
- Motoring (125)
- Personal products (39)
- Clothing (54)
- Household services (47)
- Household goods (77)
- Fuel/light (45)
- Alcohol (77)

Source: *Labour Market Trends*, HMSO

Chapter Three
Costs and benefits of inflation

'*Inflation is public enemy number one.*'
Edward Heath, as British Prime Minister, January 1973

Mistaken consensus?
Since Edward Heath spoke about inflation in 1973 it has been a generally held view that the conquest of inflation is the most important task for government economic policy. Whilst this view is beginning to be challenged in all political parties, the public universally see inflation as a *bad* thing.

Economists do not share the view of inflation held by the public – inflation can be a good or bad thing for the economy. We shall review the case for and against it.

Anticipated inflation
The problems caused by inflation can depend on whether it is expected or not. If everybody knows that inflation is going to be 10 per cent this year, and it is, then firms and consumers can plan for this. Such planning does not reduce the costs of inflation to nothing, but they are very small for the moderate inflation rates experienced in the UK.

Some economists refer to the menu costs and shoe-leather costs of inflation. By the term **menu costs** is meant that, as inflation gets higher and higher, sellers have to revise their price lists. No doubt it will cost something to keep on reprinting these price lists, but even so there can be no case here for saying that inflation is a major, or even an appreciable, cost to the economy.

Shoe-leather costs can be explained as follows. With high inflation, the amount of cash we hold for day-to-day transactions is losing value all the time. If we take £400 out of an interest-bearing account, intending to spend it through the coming month, then an inflation rate of 1 per cent a month would mean that the last £20 (spent in the last week) would be worth 20p less than when it was drawn out. This would encourage people to go to the bank more often so as to leave their money earning interest for as long as possible. The time and effort spent making these journeys to the bank are the 'shoe-leather' costs.

Why do people so often think in nominal terms? Perhaps because it is easier. Yet nominal thinking leads to bad decisions. That is awkward for governments trying to devise a policy on, say, controlling inflation. Low inflation makes money illusion less costly in terms of misallocated resources, because nominal and real values are similar. On the other hand, high inflation may make it easier for real prices to change, as they sometimes must. (For instance, workers in an uncompetitive company may need to accept a cut in real pay; they may be more willing if it is disguised as a rise in money pay.)

Source: *The Economist*, 24 Dec. 1994/5 Jan. 1995

Unanticipated inflation

- Confusion in the price mechanism

As we saw in Chapter 1, the **price mechanism** provides signals to firms and consumers on what to produce and purchase. When the price level changes owing to inflation, the price signals become confused. *The economic damage sustained during this transition arises from our inability to distinguish between changes in aggregate price level and changes in relative prices.*

Thus if producers see that customers are prepared to pay more for their products (i.e. product prices are rising), should they interpret this as an increase in the demand for their products and increase their production, as the price mechanism would suggest; or should they assume that all prices and wages are changing by the same amount and thus their product is no more in demand than before?

What is being suggested is that inflation causes confusion by making it difficult for economic agents to perceive correctly changes in relative prices.

- **Uncertainty**

Unanticipated inflation gives rise to **uncertainty** about the future, so firms are unsure about the prospective real return on investment. The overall effect of this is to lower the level of investment in the economy, reducing the productive potential of the economy. Overall output may not fall, but the cost of lost output and of unemployment is measured in terms of the level that could have been reached.

Consumers' confidence is also affected by inflation. If households are unsure how fast prices are changing they are unsure about the real purchasing power of their incomes. Their reaction is often to reduce purchases of goods and services. The result is a fall in demand for goods and services and a consequent reduction in output and employment. This means either that we must keep inflation low enough not to be an important consideration, or we must be extremely convincing in our forecasts of inflation.

- **Income and wealth distributions**

Some people feel that they have carefully planned their lives, saved, invested in pension schemes and generally acted responsibly only to find that the value of their hard-earned savings and pensions has been eroded by unforeseen increases in the price level. If price level doubles their pensions and savings lose half their value.

With regard to pensioners, it is quite difficult to find anyone on a truly fixed income. Many pensions, including state pensions, are **index-linked**. If the pensioners' price index goes up by 10 per cent, then the pensions go up by that percentage. That is one reason why the government is so keen to get an accurate measure of retail price inflation.

Those who fear that their savings will be eroded can equally be reassured. When inflation occurs, the interest rates on savings deposits rise to cover the loss of value due to inflation and to pay the normal interest rate too. Of course it is not possible always to keep interest rates absolutely in line with inflation but, by and large, if the price mechanism is working properly, there should be no loss of value of savings from this source.

There are important **redistribution effects** in certain circumstances. Lenders have tended to lose out to borrowers, because the money repaid by the borrower buys far less than when it was lent. Consider the example of a house bought for £5000 in 1968 with a 100 per cent mortgage over 25 years. By 1993 the homeowner had repaid £16 000, but the house is now worth £120 000 – the borrower has clearly gained from the transaction. The lender can try to protect the value of their capital by raising interest rates when inflation rises, but in this (real) example would have done better to buy the house personally.

Another redistribution occurs between the young and the old. Older people tend to hold more assets denominated in money terms, such as building society accounts, and during periods of high inflation these often attract a negative real interest – inflation is higher than the rate of interest paid. The young, on the other hand, tend to be *net borrowers* and are charged a low real interest rate, so benefit from the inflation. Although retirement pensions are index-linked, earnings have consistently outpaced inflation, so those in work, the young, find their real incomes rising faster than the old (from the year 2000 state old-age pensions will be increased in line with earnings to account for this).

- International competitiveness

A somewhat stronger argument for controlling inflation lies not within the economy but outside it. As the price level in the UK rises, UK goods become more and more expensive. In other countries, too, prices may be increasing; but if the UK inflation rate exceeds the rates elsewhere, then UK goods will become progressively less and less competitive compared with those other countries. This loss of **competitiveness** leads to a loss of export sales and an increase in imports. The demand for UK goods declines both at home and abroad, so UK workers are laid off and factories close.

This loss of competitiveness may be offset by a change in **exchange rates,** the price of one currency in terms of another. If our exchange rate falls (the pound devalues), at the same rate as our price level rises, then our goods will keep constant export prices and leave foreign demand for our goods unchanged.

In some circumstances the exchange rate has been determined by free markets, however this is not always possible. In Chapter 7 we shall see that at times the UK government has used the exchange rate as part of its anti-inflation policy and so devaluation is not possible.

- A strain on the market mechanism

It is possible that if the price mechanism is working well enough it can maintain relative prices at their 'correct' levels, revise interest rates so that there is no tendency to penalize lenders over borrowers, and correct exchange rates so that there is no loss of international price competitiveness.

This is placing a huge burden on the price mechanism and many would argue that it is far too heavy. The price mechanism simply cannot keep up with anything more than very moderate rates of inflation.

Similarly exchange rates, even when they are free to float, are influenced by capital flows and expected capital gains as well as price level, and simply do not change to maintain our international price competitiveness. UK exporters complain that inflation therefore leads to their losing sales and/or profits to low-inflation countries.

- Fiscal drag

Our system of income tax is not designed for an inflationary economy. Typically the amount of income tax we pay depends on our nominal (money) incomes, and the amount of capital gains tax depends on the increase in the nominal value of our assets. Consider, for example, a tax system in which we pay no income tax if our annual income is below, say, £4000; we then pay tax at a rate of 25 per cent for the next £20 000 and then at 40 per cent for the rest. Income tax paid by someone earning £60 000 per annum would be £19 400, which is 32.3 per cent of their income.

Now assume that inflation occurs and price level doubles. Incomes double too, so that the £60 000 becomes £120 000 – remember all prices have been doubled so the real value of this pre-tax income has not changed. The income tax paid now, however, will be £43 400, which is 36.2 per cent of income. Thus the tax we pay increases simply as a result of inflation, even when there is no change in the structure of tax rates or in our real pre-tax income. This is **fiscal drag**.

The effect is more dramatic for low-income families. If the income before inflation were just £4000, then no income tax would be paid; but after inflation this £4000 would double to £8000 and there would be a liability for £1000 in income tax, and so the real post-tax income would have fallen by 12.5 per cent.

Of course, the Chancellor of the Exchequer receives greater and greater tax revenues as inflation proceeds – this effect is called **fiscal boost** – but not everyone would like to see greater public revenues at the expense of the poorer members of our economy.

To take account of the effect of inflation, the Chancellor can change the amount people can earn before they pay tax. In most budgets the Chancellor raises the tax threshold by the rate of inflation or more, but there have been occasions when this has not been done, for example in November 1994.

Indexation

The changing of tax thresholds in line with inflation is known as **indexation**. Any price or value may be linked to a price index such as the RPI and adjusted in line with movements in the index.

If all prices, wages and values were fully index-linked then some economists argue that we could ignore the effects of inflation. For example wage negotiations could ignore the rate of inflation because wage rates would rise automatically. Instead they could concentrate on changing the real value of those wages.

The required effort and cost of indexing all prices and wages would be considerable, especially if done frequently to avoid effects such as fiscal drag. Indexation could also obscure relative price changes, and so would not solve the problem of reduced efficiency in the price mechanism and it could also just build inflation into the system. It is argued by many that it is better and cheaper to keep inflation to a low level by economic policy.

Inflation: A good thing?

Some economists claim that mild inflation is positively beneficial to the economy. They argue that when we have some inflation it is easier for relative prices to adjust smoothly in response to market forces. This is because some prices and wages are very difficult to reduce in money terms. Trade unions resist cuts in money wages but seem to be less worried about cuts in real wages which come about when money wages rise slower than the price level. Thus when there is inflation real wages can be reduced without the need to decrease money wage rates or reduce employment.

To see how this works, consider a market which is signalling a surplus of lawyers and a shortage of accountants. According to our theory the salaries of lawyers should fall relative to those of accountants. It turns out to be quite difficult to persuade lawyers (and others in surplus professions) to take cuts in salaries. There are wage contracts and agreements which cannot easily be broken. But, if we had a mild inflation (say 3 per cent a year) we could gradually reduce the real salaries of lawyers by simply not compensating them for the inflation. Thus mild inflation actually eases the price mechanism.

That is all very well, say other economists, but mild inflation is likely to turn into hyperinflation and destroy the currency. Therefore, they say, have none of it. The facts, however, lend scant support to this claim. There have been many inflations but very few have ever led to the destruction of a currency.

Deflation

Rather unusually, **deflation** has become an issue again in the late 1990s. Deflation is the persistent *fall* in the general price level – that is the reverse of inflation.

Deflation can present dangers to an economy, equally it can bring benefits. Deflation can be beneficial when it is due to rising productivity from increased efficiency and new technology. The world is better off in real terms. It can be bad for an economy when it is due to a slump in aggregate demand and a fall in the money supply, as happened in the 1930s during the 'Great Depression'.

There is evidence that deflation is becoming a danger, but it is not clear how much of one. There is improved productivity due to advances in information technology, deregulation of markets and falling commodity prices. There is also evidence of an increasing gap between potential and actual output in both developed and developing economies – an **output gap** – which may indicate an impending general slump.

It is not quite as simple as saying that the costs and benefits of deflation are the reverse of inflation, but that is a useful guide. For example, borrowers find the real value of their debt rising during deflation and that could cause problems for heavily endebted firms and households.

The next edition of this book may have to deal more seriously with the phenomenon that many thought had gone away forever. The graph in Figure 7 shows how the prospect of deflation has been taken more seriously in recent years.

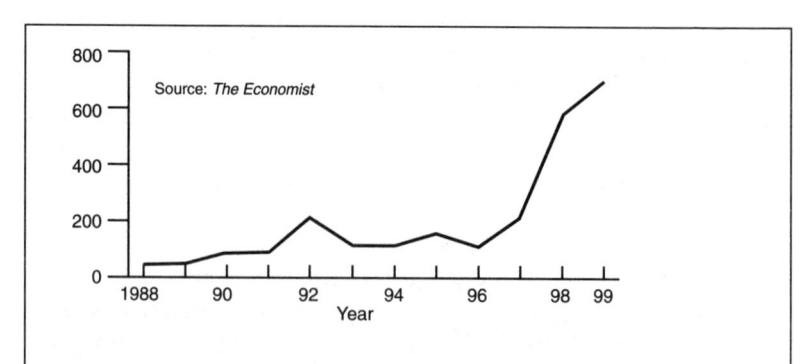

Figure 7 The D-word index: number of *Financial Times and Wall Street Journal* articles mentioning deflation

KEY WORDS

Anticipated inflation	Competitiveness
Menu costs	Exchange rates
Shoe-leather costs	Fiscal drag
Unanticipated inflation	Fiscal boost
Price mechanism	Indexation
Uncertainty	Deflation
Index-linked	Output gap
Redistribution effects	

Further reading

Anderton, A., Unit 93 in *Economics*, 2nd edn, Causeway Press, 1995.

Davies, B., Hale, G., Smith, C. and Tiller, H., Chapter 24 in *Investigating Economics*, Macmillan, 1996.

Heather, K., Chapter 15 in *Understanding Economics*, 2nd edn, Harvester Wheatsheaf, 1997.

Heathfield, D. and Russell, M., Chapter 16 in *Modern Economics*, 2nd edn, Harvester Wheatsheaf, 1992.

Useful website

The Economist: www.economist.com

Essay questions

1. Assess whether it is desirable to have a low and stable rate of inflation. [40 marks] [Oxford 1997]
2. (a) Distinguish between the effects of anticipated and unanticipated inflation. [10 marks]
   (b) Discuss whether a government should aim for zero inflation. [15 marks]

Data response question

This task is based on a question set by the OCR board in June 1998. Study Tables A and B and then answer the questions that follow.

Inflation and UK Monetary Policy

Table A Index of UK retail prices (1985 = 100)

Year	Index	Year	Index
1986	103.4	1991	141.8
1987	107.7	1992	146.4
1988	113.0	1993	148.7
1989	121.8	1994	152.4
1990	133.3	1995	157.1

Table B Inflation in selected countries (percentage change in consumer prices from previous year)

	1975	1984	1993
Germany	5.9	2.4	4.1
Japan	11.8	2.2	1.3
UK	24.2	5.0	1.6
USA	9.1	4.3	3.0
Industrial countries	11.2	4.7	2.7
World	12.2	10.6	13.0

1. Inflation in the UK, during the period 1985–95, was at its highest in 1990, and at its lowest in 1993. What evidence in Table A supports this statement? [2 marks]
2. An alternative way of measuring inflation is to consider how the pound loses real value over time. Thus, taking £1 in 1965 as the basis for comparison, this was worth 47.6p in 1975, 15.9p in 1985 and just 9.6p in 1995.
   (a) Explain how inflation and the real domestic value of a currency are related. [2 marks]
   (b) In which ten-year period between 1965 and 1995 did UK prices rise most rapidly? Explain your answer. [3 marks]
3. The UK government responded to the rising inflation of the late 1980s by taking drastic deflationary measures. The result was that total output in real terms, after several years of rapid growth, actually fell in 1991 and 1992, and did not reach its 1990 level until 1994. How might an economist explain: (i) the boom period of the late 1980s; (ii) the downturn in the UK economy in the early 1990s? [5 marks]
4. (a) Use the information in Table B to compare the UK's inflation performance with that of other countries. [3 marks]
   (b) Discuss the possible consequences of this inflation performance for the UK's overseas trade position. [5 marks]

Chapter Four
Conflicting views on the causes of inflation

'*Put all economists end to end and they would still not reach a conclusion.*'
Anonymous

The view of economists expressed in the quotation is often heard in the speeches of politicians and in the popular press. People usually want to be told 'the answer' and are frustrated either when no single answer is available, or various alternatives are offered. This problem arises in economics because we simply do not know exactly how some aspects of the economy work, and when economists form different views there is a debate, or controversy. The cause of inflation is one area of economics where there are strongly held, but opposing, views.

The existence of a controversy makes economics a difficult subject for students because they are used to certainty (for example, not many people studying for A level Physics debate what force gravity exerts). Students of economics must be able to understand that there are equally valid alternative views in economics, and then be able to look at the available data. That is an important part of what economists do and it is a vital skill to learn. It is also worth remembering that *all* the alternative theories might be wrong!

In this chapter we shall be looking at the *three main theories* put forward as the cause of inflation, and in Chapter 5 we shall look at some of the inflation data for the UK.

Monetarist theories

Monetarists believe that the fundamental cause of inflation is an unmerited rise in the money supply. A merited rise in the money supply would occur if the money supply increased in line with output. For example, Professor Milton Friedman, who was the most public proponent of monetarism, is often quoted as saying:

'*Inflation is always and everywhere a monetary phenomenon.*'

The basis of the monetarist case is the quantity theory of money.

- **The quantity equation**

The **quantity equation** is expressed as:

$$M \times V = P \times Y$$

where M is the quantity of money in circulation, V is the velocity of circulation, P is the general price level, and Y is the quantity of real goods and services produced in the time period, usually one year.

The equation is more properly written as $M \times V = P \times T$, where T is the number of transactions. The data on this are not easily available and economists usually use current output as an approximation. We shall use Y rather than T, but you may treat the two forms as similar.

The left-hand side of the quantity equation tells us how much money is in circulation (M) and how often each note or coin changes hands in each period – that is, how fast the money circulates, hence the term 'velocity' (V). If there are 1000 £1 coins in circulation and each changes hands five times in the course of a year, then the velocity of circulation is 5 and M × V is equal to £5000. This tells us that firms', households' and government expenditure has been £5000 during the year. Notice that doubling the velocity of circulation with the same money stock has the same effect on the price level as doubling the supply of money.

The right-hand side of the equation tells us that the value of goods and services supplied is equal to the amount of real goods and services produced (Y) multiplied by the average price they are sold at (P). In other words P × Y gives us the money value, or nominal value, of national output. If the price level were to double then so would the money value of national output.

- **From an equation to a theory**

The quantity equation above must always be true, because it is nothing more than what is called an **accounting identity** – the value of expenditure on goods and services demanded and supplied equals the value of output. When looking back on a year the quantity equation must hold. The monetarist case is that inflation is caused by *unwarranted* increases in the money supply and it is their assumptions about the quantity equation which makes it a theory of the cause of inflation – the Quantity Theory.

Monetarists assume that the velocity of circulation is fixed, at least in the short term. This is because the rate at which money circulates is determined by habit and institutional arrangements – for example how often workers are paid. The more often workers are paid, the faster money could circulate. In practice such arrangements do not change very often, hence the assumption that V is fixed. In consequence any rise in the money supply cannot be offset by a fall in the velocity of circulation on the left-hand side of the equation, implying that the value of the right-hand side of the equation (P × Y) must rise following a rise in the money supply.

Of course the rise on the right-hand side of the equation could be taken up by a rise in real output (Y). Monetarists rule out this possibility by assuming that real output is also fixed. Thus any rise in the money supply feeds directly through into higher prices, as the example below demonstrates.

Assume that the money supply is initially £1000 and the velocity of circulation is 5. The level of output is 5000 units and the average price level is £1. The quantity equation for this economy is:

$$M \times V = P \times Y$$
$$1000 \times 5 = 1 \times 5000.$$

Now suppose that the money supply doubles. The velocity of circulation is assumed to be fixed at 5 and the level of output fixed at 5000 units. For the equation to balance the average price level must double (from £1 to £2):

$$2000 \times 5 = 2 \times 5000.$$

When the constraints of stable velocity and output are imposed on the quantity equation the equation is known as the **Fisher equation** or quantity theory.

- ### Introducing time into the quantity theory
In fact monetarists accept that both the velocity of circulation and the level of real output do vary. The crucial points they make are that:

- velocity does not vary very much in *the short term* and can be treated as fixed, and
- real output can vary in the short run, but will return to a long-run equilibrium level – sometimes known as **long-run supply** or the **natural rate of output** – quite quickly.

Thus in a short time any rise in the money supply will feed through into higher prices.

Milton Friedman himself suggested that the exact timing of the process will be difficult to predict, but gave a rough guide:

- Following a rise in the money supply there will first be a rise in the level of output around nine months to one year later.

- A further nine months to one year after that, output will return to its long-run equilibrium rate and prices will rise to accommodate the higher money supply.

Thus the entire process takes time, and in the UK the monetarist view has often been represented as there being approximately a two-year lag between a rise in the money supply and a rise in the price level.

The process can be illustrated in the aggregate demand and aggregate supply model which is debated in the article quoted from the *Independent on Sunday*.

- **Monetarist inflation in the aggregate demand and aggregate supply model**

Following a rise in the money supply, consumers will find they have more money available to spend and they will raise their demand for real goods and services. This shifts the aggregate demand curve to the right, from AD_1 to AD_2 in Figure 8. Firms will respond to this increase in aggregate demand and raise output, moving along the short-run aggregate supply curve, from point A to point B.

This rise in output causes the economy to exceed the long-run

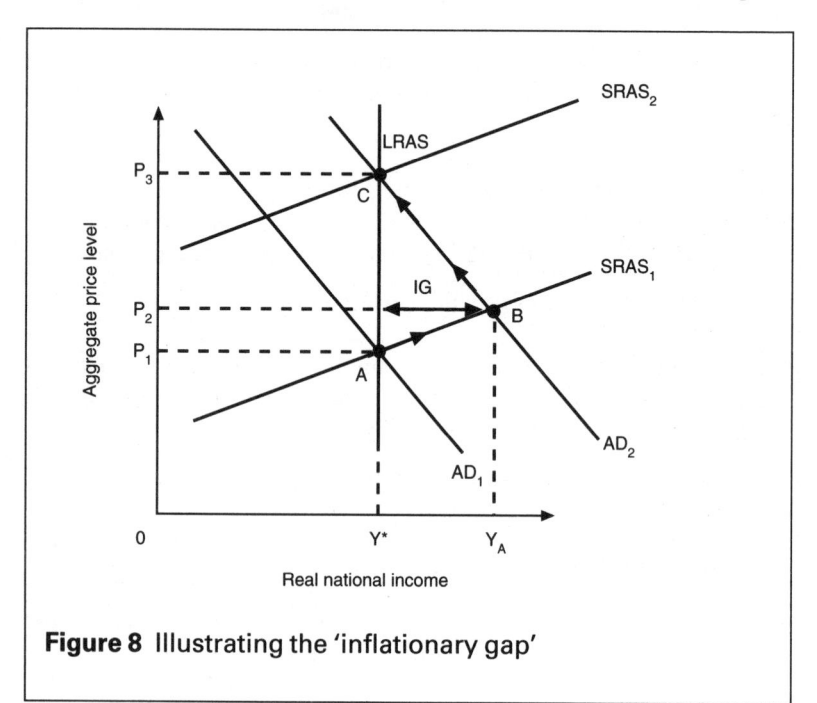

Figure 8 Illustrating the 'inflationary gap'

Interview

MILTON FRIEDMAN

Milton Friedman has achieved a status sometimes found among pop singers or Middle East dictators, seldom among economists. He has become a hero, or a demon, in places he has rarely, if ever visited.

In Britain, a country he has only occasionally called on, his name still conjures up, depending on your viewpoint; the smack of firm government and the conquest of double-digit inflation; or rocketing interest rates, gross unemployment and the scything of swathes of British industry. He is unfailingly associated with the early Thatcher years, and with the M-word.

At his zenith, in the sixties and seventies, Friedman was the leader of the Chicago school of free-market economics, which prepared the way for Reaganomics and Thatcherism. (Eighty per cent of the economists in the Reagan administrations studied under Friedman.) Now, unlike John Maynard Keynes, he has lived, in the words of a younger US economist, 'to see his children die,' to see his ideas 'tried and abandoned and then disputed and mangled by the next generation of economists'.

Monetarism is not necessarily Friedman's most important contribution to the history of ideas, but it remains his most celebrated idea and, mangled and disputed though it may be, it refuses to go away.

His original conception of monetarism, he insists, was not applied properly in either Britain or the US. The plan was for governments, like Ulysses strapped to the mast, to set an unbreachable limit on monetary growth; in practice, in both London and Washington, he says, the politicians and bureaucrats could not resist interfering with the rudder. Instead of shrinking the supply in money directly (by restricting the supply of currency and credit to banks), the Thatcher government and the US Federal Reserve tinkered with interest rates – a Friedman no-no – in an attempt to achieve the same result.

The bureaucrats themselves and post-Friedman economists have a somewhat different memory. They say the theory was tried as well as it could have been tried; but Friedman over-simplified the difficulties of measuring and controlling the money supply. For Christopher Dow, Director for Economics in the Bank of England during the early Thatcher years, the very name of Friedman produces an audible intake of breath over the phone. 'Friedman had an unrealistic idea about how you could control the volume of money,' he says. 'He thought it was like a tap and you just turned it off. If you didn't stop the growth of money, you hadn't turned the tap far enough. The world doesn't work that way any more.'

The rising star of US economics today, Paul Krugman of the Massachusetts Institute of Technology, says: 'By the end of the 1980s, Friedman had made himself frankly ridiculous to professional economists. He was continually predicting outrageous inflation and severe slumps, based on monetary movements that strayed from his chosen path. And they didn't happen in the way he predicted.'

Friedman remains unshakeable in his faith that monetarism and the other free market experiments of the Eighties, in the US and Britain, did not fail: they succeeded in part but then fell back, through corruption of principle, or lack of nerve.

Independent on Sunday, 26 July 1992

equilibrium level of output (Y*), given by LRAS in Figure 8, and what is known as an **inflationary gap** occurs, shown as IG in the figure. An inflationary gap is the difference between actual and long-run output when aggregate demand and short-run aggregate supply intersect to the right of LRAS.

As a consequence of the rise in aggregate demand, from AD_1 to AD_2, firms hire more labour and work above normal full-capacity. As can be seen in Figure 8, this causes a rise in costs and so the average price level rises from P_1 to P_2. As prices rise the quantity of money in circulation can buy fewer goods and services – a move to the left along the new aggregate demand curve AD_2. Furthermore, workers demand higher money wages in order to continue to work the hours required to produce the higher level of output as higher prices have reduced the real value of their wages. The short-run aggregate supply curve moves to the left as money wage rates rise, eventually reaching $SRAS_2$ at point C. The economy has gradually returned to the long-run equilibrium rate of output (Y*), but at a higher price level (P_3).

Notice that the rise in the money supply first caused a rise in demand. Hence this form of inflation is known as **demand-pull inflation**.

The Keynesian view

In his book *The General Theory of Employment, Interest and Money*, published in 1936, Keynes rejected the monetarists' view of how the economy works. Keynes believed that the level of real output was determined by the level of aggregate demand, and that the price mechanism would not automatically bring the economy back to a long-run equilibrium level of output that was close to full employment.

In Keynesian theory money is held in speculative balances as well as for transactions, so M in the quantity equation is not 'given' by money supply. Inflation is caused by excessive aggregate demand, as shown in Figure 9, but this is not due necessarily to a rise in the money supply, but to the actions of firms, households and governments wishing to spend more than the economy can produce.

- Capacity output

Keynesians do not believe that the level of output in the economy is fixed. Rather they believe that it will fluctuate according to the level of aggregate demand. In an open economy aggregate demand is the sum of consumers' expenditure (C), firms' investment expenditure (I), government expenditure (G) and the demand for exports less the demand for imports (X minus M). A rise in any of these components of expenditure will shift the aggregate demand curve to the right.

Figure 9 Keynesian aggregate demand and supply model

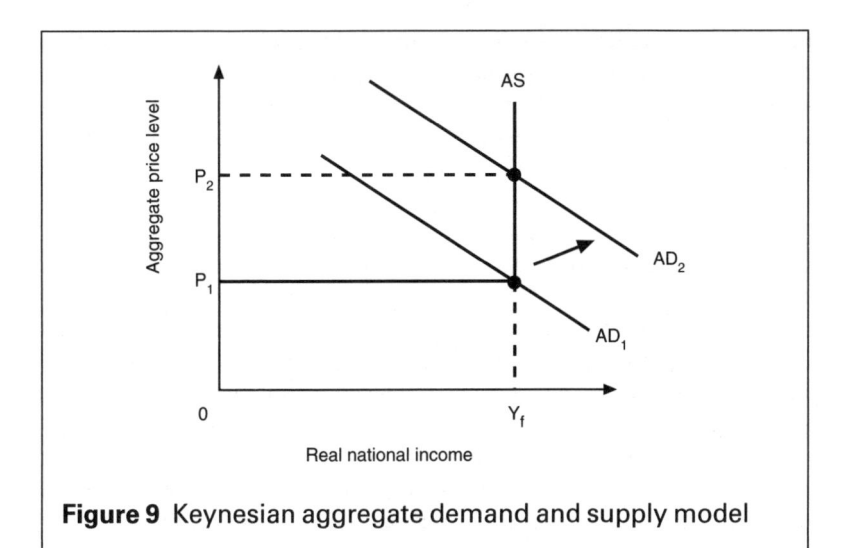

There will be levels of aggregate demand that are not sufficient to employ all of the resources and workers in the economy, and so unemployment will result. At higher levels of aggregate demand the economy will have insufficient resources to produce the goods to meet this demand, and that is when inflation occurs. There is a level of output at which all resources are fully employed – *this is the full-capacity output of the economy* where there would be unemployment. As the components of aggregate demand (C + I + G + [X – M]) are often determined independently, there is no reason why the level of aggregate demand should end up at the full-employment level.

In the simple Keynesian model, when the level of aggregate demand exceeds the real output of the economy at its full-employment level the only way to accommodate extra aggregate demand is for prices to rise. In other words, the rise in price means the given level of aggregate demand can purchase fewer real goods and services. This is shown in the aggregate demand and supply model in Figure 9. The rise in aggregate demand beyond AD_1 means that the economy moves on to the vertical part of the aggregate supply curve to a higher price level.

- Inflation and unemployment

Figure 9 suggests that the price level remains the same until full employment (Y_f) is reached; i.e. there is unemployment only at levels of output below Y_f with no inflation. After the level of aggregate demand exceeds Y_f there is inflation and no further rise in output.

This is too simplistic a view, and all Keynesians would accept that there would be some moderate inflation before full employment is reached and the rate of inflation would rise as full employment is approached. The higher the level of aggregate demand, the higher the rate of inflation. This is illustrated by the aggregate supply curve in Figure 10.

Figure 10 shows three shifts of the aggregate demand curve, the first two due to identical rises in the level of government expenditure (ΔG). In the first case, the shift from AD_1 to AD_2 causes both a rise in output and a fall in unemployment and raises the price level. The second movement of the aggregate demand curve causes a smaller rise in output and a larger rise in the price level. The shape of the aggregate supply curve has caused the difference between these two changes.

As real output rises, the economy begins to run short of certain resources (perhaps skilled labour), and some resources, such as machines, run at full capacity. From microeconomics we know that in the short run as output expands the law of diminishing marginal returns sets in and firms' marginal costs rise. Thus as output rises towards full employment there is a slow rise in the price level as some resources reach capacity, causing a 'bottleneck'. The closer to full employment the economy becomes, the more bottlenecks there are in the economy and costs rise even faster.

In Figure 10, after full employment is reached, any increase in aggregate demand leads only to a price level rise and no change in output.

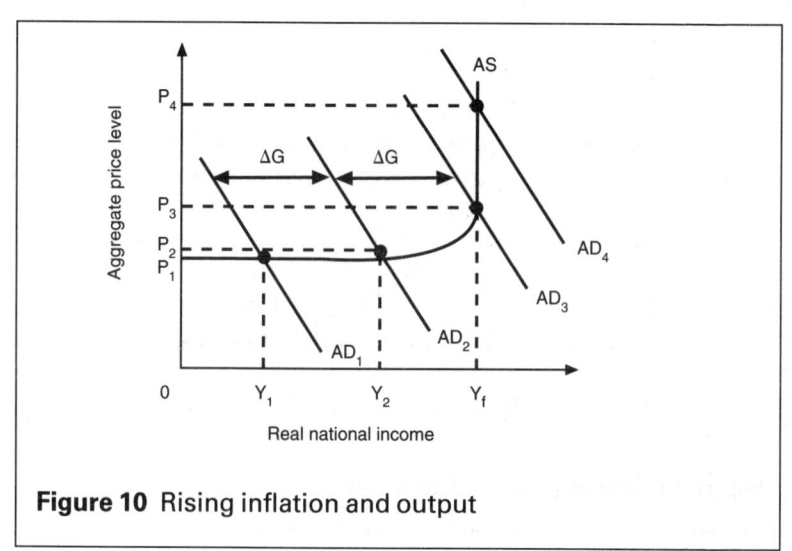

Figure 10 Rising inflation and output

Conflicting views on the causes of inflation

The Keynesians would, therefore, expect to see a strong relationship between the level of output and the rate of inflation. As output and employment of labour are so closely linked, the relationship between unemployment and inflation should be equally clear. Such a relationship was discovered by A. W. Phillips.

- **The Phillips curve**

Phillips examined the relationship between the rate of change of money wage rates, wage inflation, and the level of unemployment in the UK spanning the years 1861–1957. This relationship is shown in Figure 11 and is known as the **Phillips curve**.

Phillips found that when unemployment was high, wage inflation was low. As the economy expanded and unemployment fell, then wage inflation rose – slowly at first but faster and faster as unemployment fell further and further. This *nonlinear relationship* supports the view of the aggregate supply curve represented in Figure 10. The level of unemployment is a measure of how close the economy is to full-employment (capacity) output, and as this is approached so prices will begin to rise.

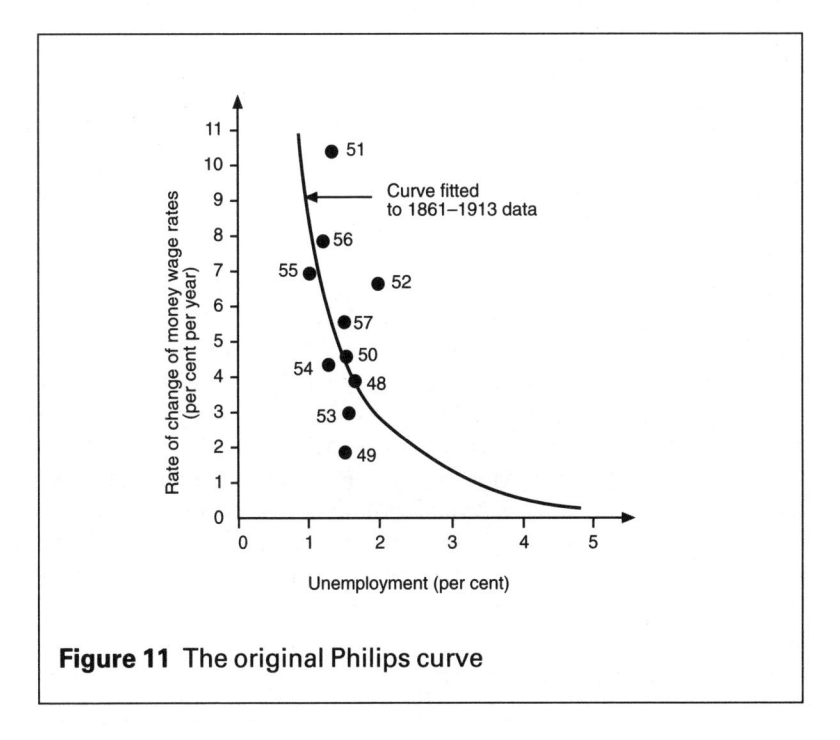

Figure 11 The original Philips curve

The Phillips curve is drawn in terms of wage rates and unemployment, *whereas we are interested in the causes of price inflation, not wage inflation.* The next step is therefore to forge a link between the money wage rate and the aggregate price index.

The link between the rate of wage inflation and price inflation is due to the large proportion of total costs of production made up by labour costs. If the wage rate rises, then firms will have to raise prices to protect profit margins *unless they can cut costs in some other way.* As full employment is approached labour becomes more scarce and it is necessary to offer higher wages to attract the required workers. At such times the position of trade unions becomes much stronger and they may succeed in their attempts to negotiate higher wage rates for their members, free from the threat of unemployment. Even if a firm has a low proportion of direct labour costs as part of total costs, it will find the cost of inputs rising as its suppliers are obliged to raise their wage rates. These cost rises must be passed on to customers to maintain profitability.

The only relief for firms comes in the form of **labour productivity** gains. Labour productivity is a measure of the output per employee and this increases steadily over time. Any rise in productivity can be set against wage rises, and so the rise in the price level will be offset by a rise in labour productivity.

- Demand-pull again

The Keynesian view of the cause of inflation is also that it is due initially to a rise in aggregate demand. *However, the cause of the rise in aggregate demand and the process by which inflation proceeds differs from the monetarist view.*

The rise in aggregate demand is due not necessarily to a rise in the money supply, but to any of the components of aggregate demand. This leads to a rise in costs which are then passed on in the form of higher prices. The rate at which prices rise depends on how close the economy is to full employment, whereas in the monetarist argument the rise in the money supply always leads to a rise in the price level.

The strong evidence provided by the discovery of the Phillips curve led to a widespread view that the Keynesian explanation of inflation was correct. As we shall see in the next chapter, in the mid-1960s the Phillips relationship seemed to have broken down.

Cost-push inflation

Most people would say that it is obvious that prices are related to costs of production. If these costs rise then prices will rise too. This is the essence of **cost-push inflation**. There are two main sources of rising costs that we can identify:

- the UK labour market
- import prices.

- **The labour market**

In the cost-push theory of inflation, wages are determined in labour markets where ideally employers compete among themselves for workers (which keeps wages from falling too low) and workers compete among themselves for jobs (which prevents wages rising too high).

But labour markets are imperfect markets, especially when there is a unionized sector. Trades unions have many purposes, but an important aspect of their work is wage negotiations. Instead of each worker striking a bargain with an employer, a trade union negotiates for all its members together. Presenting a common front confers market power to workers, and so employers have to pay up or do without unionized labour altogether. Since labour, like energy, is a widely used and essential input into all productive enterprises, this increase in wages will force up costs and so force up the price level too. The technical name for the market power being described here is **monopoly power.**

This view of inflation, based on the increasing market power of sellers, is clearly to do with costs increasing even when there is no encouragement to do so from the demand side of the market. It is therefore 'cost-push inflation'.

- **Import prices**

As the UK is an open economy, the prices charged by foreign firms for their goods and services affects the UK price level. In 1997 the UK imported £183 billion of goods, almost one-third of gross domestic product (GDP), making the price of imported goods a very important component of our aggregate price level.

Trade is carried out between countries who (at least in the UK's case for the foreseeable future) make use of different currencies. To sell goods in another country it is necessary to price those goods in the currency of that country so the buyer understands the price. The **exchange rate** plays a crucial role in setting the quoted price.

Suppose a German car manufacturer charges a price of 40 000 deutschemarks (DM) for its product. If the exchange rate for the pound to the DM is £1:3DM the car is priced at £13 333, but if the exchange rate falls to £1:2DM it is priced at £20 000. Thus the UK price level will rise. As Figure 12 shows, the value of the pound varied over a range of nearly 10 per cent in the first ten months of 1998. (The ERI is a trade-weighted index of 20 countries' exchange rates against sterling. The broad ERI is constructed using 49 countries' exchange rates.) The downward trend in the exchange rate since March 1998 will lead to a rise in the RPI.

Perhaps the best known example of the influence of import prices on inflation is that in the market for crude oil. This example also illustrates the effect of market power when held by producers. There being only a few big suppliers of oil, it became possible for them to collude rather than compete. Instead of each oil producer negotiating a price per barrel with oil users, the major oil producers and exporters worked together forming a near monopoly, known as a 'cartel'. This cartel is called OPEC – the Organization of Petroleum Exporting Countries – and together they fix a price for oil and present oil users with that price.

Oil is essential to most developed economies, so producers have users 'over a barrel'. They have to pay up or perish. If the price of oil increases then so too will the prices of those commodities which depend on it. Thus there will be a rise in the general price level whatever the level of the money supply or aggregate demand might be, as there was following the oil price rises of 1974/75 and 1979/80.

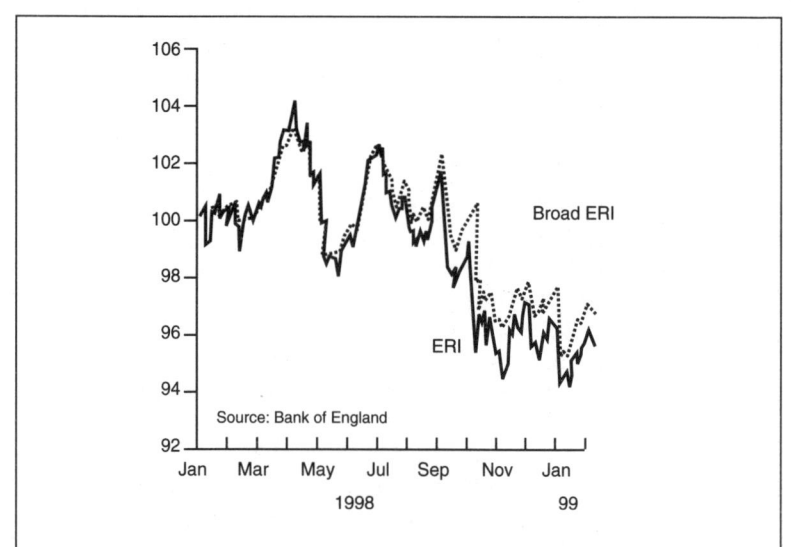

Figure 12 Sterling effective exchange rate during 1998 (2 January 1998 = 100)

Although the prices of other commodities do not have the same dramatic effect on inflation as oil, any rise in their prices can feed through into higher retail prices.

- **Cost-push inflation in the AD/AS model**

When the costs of production in the economy rise – say, owing to a rise in money wage rates – the short-run aggregate supply curve will shift upwards. *You will recall that in the monetarist and Keynesian theories the aggregate demand curve moved first.* The effect of a rise in production costs across the economy as a whole is shown in Figure 13.

Assuming that the economy begins in long-run equilibrium at real output Y_1 and a price level of P_1, a general rise in production costs leads the short-run aggregate supply curve to shift to the left, from $SRAS_1$ to $SRAS_2$. This leads to a lower level of output, Y_2, and a higher price level, P_2.

Domestically generated inflation and imported inflation

The analysis above helps us to distinguish between inflation that has its source within the UK and that which is outside the control of the UK. Domestically generated inflation is that which would occur in a closed

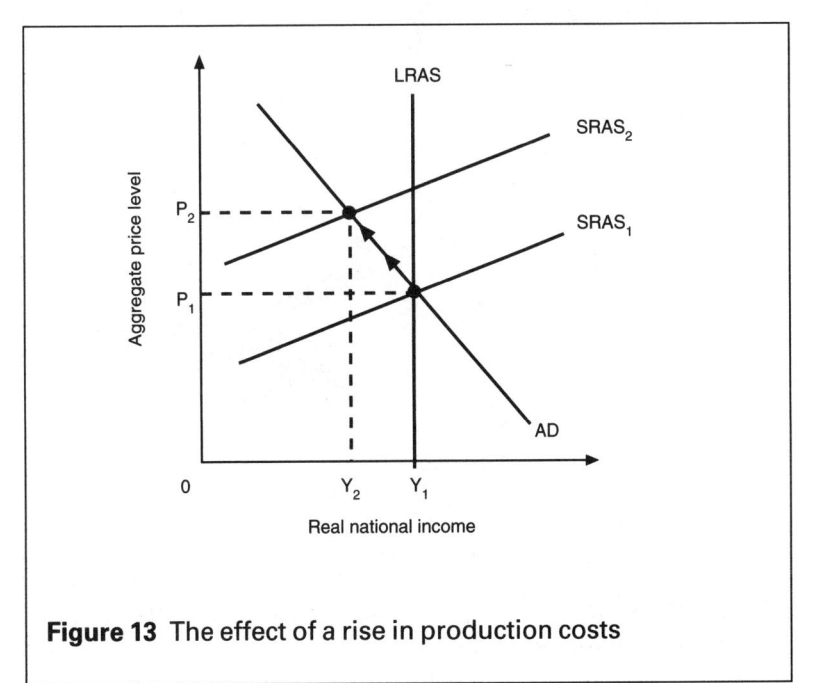

Figure 13 The effect of a rise in production costs

economy. It may be due to demand-pull or cost-push factors. For example a group of firms within the UK can act to raise prices if they have market power, like OPEC has internationally.

Figure 14 shows the influence of costs on the retail price index for the UK (some of the percentages do not sum to 100 because of rounding). The emphasis on the goods sector reflects the lack of data for the services sector, which represents 44 per cent of the RPI.

Figure 14 shows that import prices have an important effect on the goods market, mainly via raw material prices. Some services are imported, but are used almost exclusively by the corporate sector and so affect the RPI indirectly.

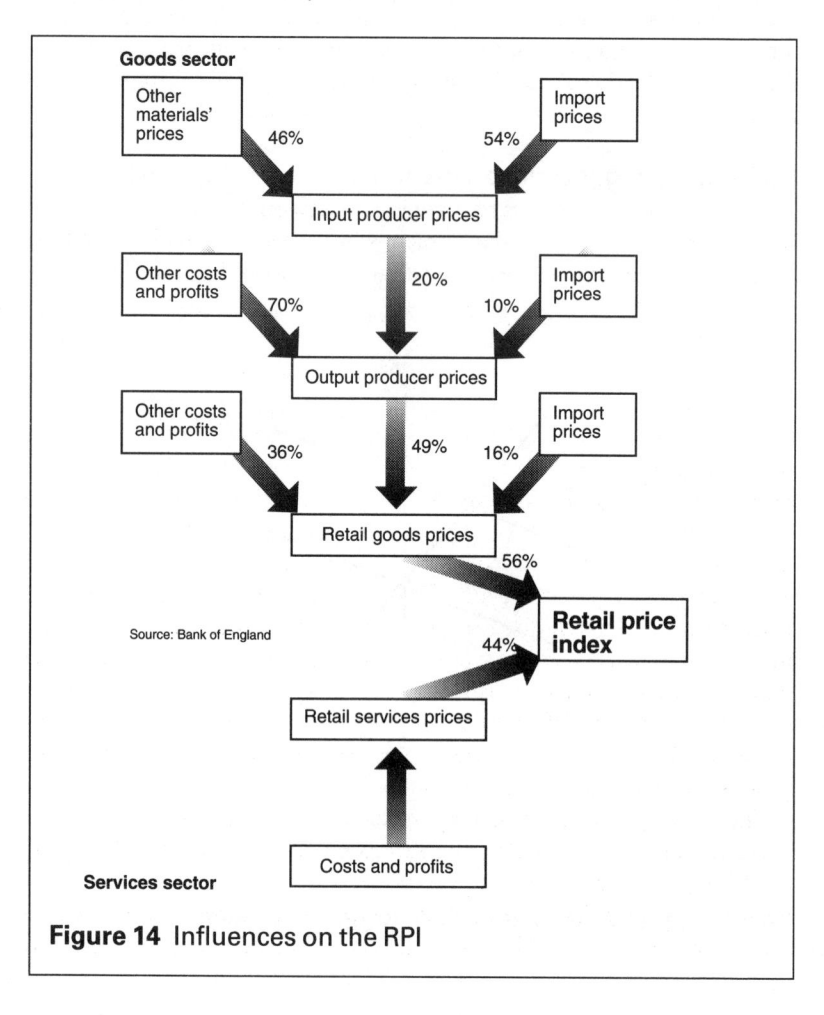

Figure 14 Influences on the RPI

It should not be inferred from Figure 14 that prices are simply made up of aggregated costs. Inflation can be caused by cost factors, such as a rise in oil prices, which raise input costs at the top and bottom of the diagram and feed into the RPI. Inflation can also be caused by demand factors, for example a rise in consumer spending, which will first affect the retail sector, putting pressure on the market for labour and feeding back through the diagram as higher costs.

Continuing inflation

The aggregate demand and supply model has, in each of the three theories we have examined, shown how there is a rise in the aggregate price level following a change in a key variable. *The model does not show continuing inflation however – rather it implies a once-and-for-all rise in the price level to a new equilibrium.*

A once-and-for-all rise in the price level is not what we defined as inflation in Chapter 1. Inflation is a *continuous* rise in the general price level. The reasons why the price level continues to rise can be numerous. For example there could be a sustained rise in the money supply in the monetarist case, or continuing rises in aggregate demand in the Keynesian case. In the case of cost-push inflation, the fall in real national output implies higher unemployment, and this may prompt the government to use fiscal policy – that is, cut taxes and increase government expenditure – to raise aggregate demand, further raising the price level.

The most common reason for continuing inflation is the effect a rise in the price level has on the behaviour of economic agents. This is often referred to as a **wage–price spiral**. The initial cause of the rising price level can be left aside; the effect of higher prices is to induce workers to ask for compensation in the form of higher money wages as they attempt to restore their previous real income. If they are successful this leads to a further rise in the price level and further calls for higher money wages. The process continues as groups of workers try to maintain their relative position in society – often referred to as maintaining **wage differentials** – where groups of workers try to maintain the same gaps between their wages and the wages of other groups, or their share of national income.

The response of the monetary authorities to a change in aggregate demand (a **demand 'shock'**) or aggregate supply (a **supply 'shock'**) is also thought to be crucial. Suppose there is a rise in wage rates due to wage rises higher than productivity gains. The aggregate supply curve moves to the left. The monetary authorities may decide to *accommodate* this supply shock by raising the money supply in order to restore real output, causing the aggregate demand curve to shift to the right and so the price level rises further. Continued **monetary accommodation** leads to continuous inflation.

If there is a demand shock the aggregate demand curve shifts to the right. The monetary authorities may decide to *validate* this rise in aggregate demand by raising the money supply as the higher level of output and prices raises the transactions demand for money. This **monetary validation** continues the rise in the price level, and any compensating shift of the aggregate supply curve to offset the original demand shock fails to return output to its original level.

Thus the behaviour of the monetary authorities is vital in the path inflation takes.

Inflation, once begun, can have many complex and interlinked reasons for continuing. It is far from easy to see the true cause during the process itself and to take action to halt the rise in the price level. For example, if the cause of inflation is due to cost-push factors, the money supply will still rise during this period in order to meet the demand for cash to settle the now higher value of transactions. Observing the money supply during this period may lead commentators to conclude that the cause of the inflation is the rise in the money supply.

The cause of inflation in the UK is a complex mix of many factors. In the next chapter we shall look at some data for the UK economy in order to discover more about the nature of UK inflation.

KEY WORDS

Monetarists	Labour productivity
Quantity equation	Cost-push inflation
Accounting identity	Monopoly power
Fisher equation	Exchange rate
Long-run supply	Wage–price spiral
Natural rate of output	Wage differentials
Inflationary gap	Demand and supply shocks
Demand-pull inflation	Monetary accommodation
Phillips curve	Monetary validation

Further reading
Anderton, A., Unit 94 in *Economics*, 2nd edn, Causeway Press, 1995.
Atkinson, B., Baker, P. and Milward, R., Chapter 12 in *Economic Policy*, Macmillan, 1996.
Atkinson, B., Livesey, F. and Milward, R., Chapter 22 in *Applied Economics*, Macmillan, 1998.
Sloman, J., Chapter 21 in *Economics*, 3rd edn, Prentice Hall, 1997.

Useful website
Bank of England: The *Inflation Report* is available at www.bankofengland.co.uk

Essay questions
1. It is often claimed that there are two sources of inflation: demand-pull and cost-push. Assess the economic consequences of a government taking action to reduce inflation without considering what is causing it. [40 marks] [Oxford 1998]
2. (a) What are the main causes of cost-push inflation? [10 marks]
   (b) Use aggregate demand and supply analysis to explain how a rise in the general price level can develp into inflation. [15 marks]

Data response question
This task is based on a question set by the University of Oxford Delegacy of Local Examinations in 1998. Read the following short extract, taken from *The Economist* of 14 December 1996. Then answer the questions that follow, using your knowledge of economics and economic analysis.

According to basic economic textbooks, there are two main types of inflation: 'cost-push' and 'demand-pull'. With costs currently showing little inclination to push prices higher – indeed, with the strong pound lowering import prices, costs may even fall – the crucial question is whether demand will pull them up.

1. Using aggregate demand and aggregate supply diagrams, distinguish between 'cost-push' and 'demand-pull' inflation. [6 marks]
2. What effect have movements in the exchange rate had on the inflation rate over the last year? [4 marks]
3. Briefly explain how fiscal policy measures can be used to reduce 'demand-pull' inflation. [8 marks]

Chapter Five
Inflation in the UK

'*We are all Keynesians now.*'
President Richard Nixon, when President of the United States of America, 1968

The breakdown of consensus
From the 1950s to the late 1960s it appeared that the Keynesian account of how the economy worked had provided economists with all they needed to know. When President Nixon uttered the famous words above, the economy had already begun to behave in a way that was inconsistent with the Keynesians' theory. There followed a period of rapid inflation that caused great concern and was not brought under control until the 1990s. In this chapter we shall look at the UK's experience of inflation and see how well the three theories examined in Chapter 4 conform to actual experience.

The breakdown of the Phillips curve
Faith in the Phillips curve, and in the Keynesian analysis of inflation, took a severe knock in the 1970s when very high inflation rates were experienced at the same time as there was very high unemployment – see Figure 15.

Between 1967 and 1975 there was an enormous rise in inflation, from 4 to 26 per cent, with little or no change in unemployment. Since 1975, wage inflation has been variable but unemployment rates have been consistently higher than in the previous period. This conjunction of high inflation and high unemployment is called **stagflation**.

Stagflation is problematic for Keynesians, because if there is high unemployment there must be deficient aggregate demand; and if there is deficient aggregate demand there can be no upward pressure on prices and wages – *therefore there can be no inflation: but there was.*

The decline in popularity of the Phillips curve was accelerated by the re-emergence of the monetarist view. Monetarists argue that the level of employment, and hence the level of unemployment, is determined by the level of **real wages,** which can be thought of as the amount of goods and services money wages will buy. This means there can be no trade-off between unemployment and money wages. Their theory certainly

Figure 15 Inflation and unemployment, 1965–98

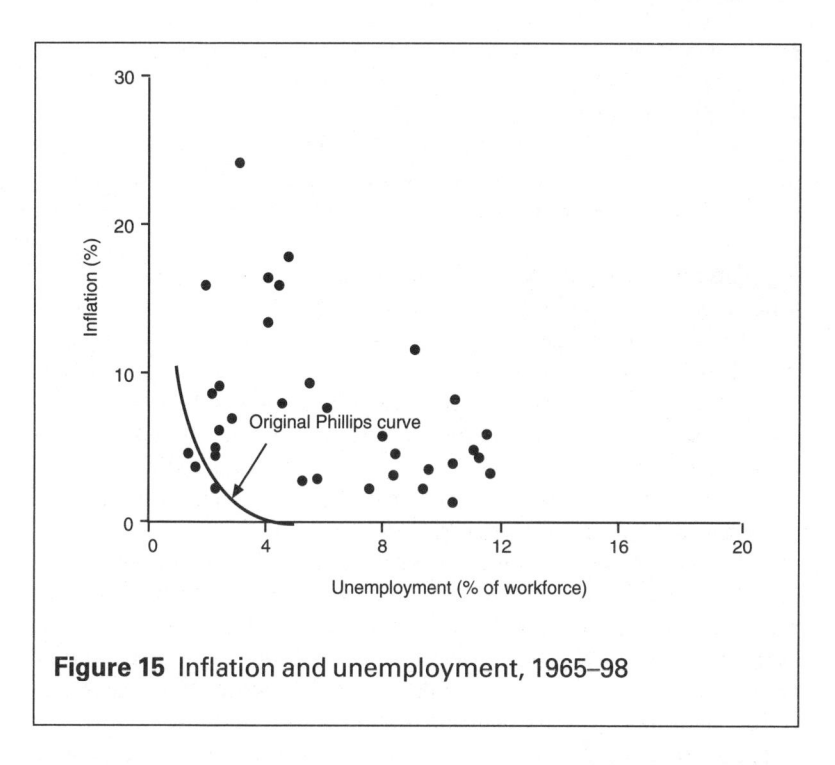

leads them to this conclusion and, after 1974, there is some empirical support for them; but there remains the evidence of the original Phillips curve.

To explain this away, monetarists suggest that workers will offer to work more if they believe their real wages have been increased. This would be the case, for example, if they thought that the price level would increase by less than their money wage increased. The argument goes as follows.

Workers, or their trades unions, are offered a 10 per cent increase in money wage and invited to sign annual employment contracts on the basis of that money wage. At this stage the workers do not know what will happen to the price level in the coming year, but if they expect it to remain constant then they will see the 10 per cent increase in money wages as a 10 per cent increase in real wages. They will offer more worker-hours and employment will increase. They will soon find out that they were wrong about price level – it actually rose by 10 per cent too – so real wages remain unchanged, but by then it is too late for them to rewrite their contracts.

The monetarists are arguing, therefore, that the Phillips curve is the result of workers forming wrong expectations about price increases. Employment, they argue, really is determined by real wage – but expected real wage rather than actual real wage.

They go on to say that eventually workers will learn from their mistakes and begin to expect price increases, and when they do the Phillips curve breaks down – just as it did in the 1970s.

- **Expectations-augmented Phillips curve**

Once workers expect 10 per cent inflation they will want a 10 per cent increase in money wages just to maintain their expected real wages. In their wage negotiations they will need 10 per cent more just to keep worker-hours (employment) at last year's level. To get them to increase worker-hours (employment) they would have to be offered a 20 per cent increase in money wages. They would then discover that inflation rose to 20 per cent rather than the expected 10 per cent and their real wage would be what it was before.

The point is that the Phillips curve depends on what workers expect future inflation rates to be. If they expect no inflation then the relationship between employment and inflation will look like the original Phillips curve; but if workers expect 10 per cent inflation then the whole curve moves up by 10 per cent. If they expect 20 per cent then the curve moves up by 20 per cent.

These 'stacked' Phillips curves are called **expectations-augmented Phillips curves** (see Figure 16) and are due to the work of monetarists such as Friedman.

- **The natural rate of unemployment**

As we have seen, employment is increased when workers underestimate inflation and is decreased when they overestimate inflation – that is what gives the Phillips curves their shapes.

If workers correctly estimated inflation – i.e. their expectations turned out to be correct – they would offer the *right* amount of labour. This *right* amount is called the **natural rate of employment** and the unemployment associated with it is called the **natural rate of unemployment**. Since this level of unemployment is the only rate compatible with correct expectations, all other combinations of unemployment and inflation rate must occur when expectations are wrong.

The Phillips 'curve' when expectations are correct is therefore a vertical straight line – often referred to as the vertical or **long-run Phillips curve**.

The vertical Phillips curve obviously occurs at the natural rate of

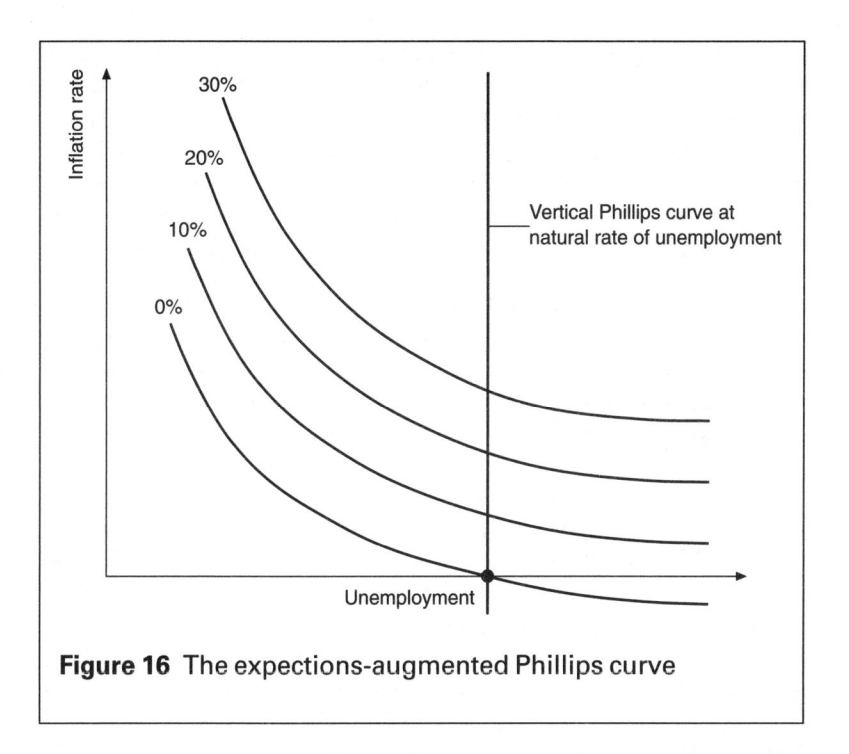

Figure 16 The expections-augmented Phillips curve

unemployment, and the natural rate can be found by examining the data on unemployment and price inflation in the original Phillips curve. That curve was constructed when workers expected an inflation rate of zero. The natural rate of unemployment would therefore be that level of unemployment at which these expectations proved correct; that is to say, at that level of unemployment at which inflation would actually be zero. When actual price inflation is zero their expectations would be correct.

Whatever the level of price expectations, the rate of unemployment where expectations are correct is still the natural rate of unemployment. At all other rates of unemployment, workers either underestimate the rate of inflation when the rate of unemployment is less than the natural rate, or overestimate the rate of inflation when unemployment is greater than the natural rate. In both cases the labour market will not be in equilibrium.

If the level of unemployment is less than the natural rate, workers will demand wage increases higher than the expected rate to maintain the required supply of labour, and this will bring about a rise in the inflation rate. When the level of unemployment is above the natural rate, the rise in money wages demanded to keep secure the required amount of labour will be less than the expected rate and the rate of inflation will fall. *Only at the natural rate of unemployment will the required rise in wage rates match the expected inflation rate, resulting in stable inflation.* Thus another name for the natural rate of unemployment is the *non-accelerating inflation rate of unemployment*, or **NAIRU**.

- The Phillips curve from 1965 to 1998

Figure 15 showed how the data on inflation and unemployment have departed from Phillips' original findings. This certainly does not support the simple Keynesian case for the cause of inflation, and the monetarists' attempts to introduce expectations into the model seem to have some support.

The question of the existence of a natural rate is less easy to settle from the data. A natural rate helps the monetarists to justify their assumption about a fixed rate of output in the quantity theory, but none seems to be evident. There have been various estimates of the natural rate of unemployment, ranging from 2.25 per cent in the 1960s to 12 per cent in the 1980s, and some evidence that the NAIRU actually moves, reducing the validity of the theory.

Money supply and the rate of inflation

The monetarist case lies not with the expectations-augmented Phillips curve, but with the relationship between the money supply and the rate of inflation. In Chapter 4 we saw that monetarists expect a strong relationship between changes in the money supply and the rate of inflation, but with about a two-year lag. The relationship is defined by the quantity theory $M \times V = P \times Y$. In Chapter 4 we stated that monetarists assume the velocity of circulation (V) and the real output (Y) to be fixed. In truth monetarists relax the assumption of fixed real output in favour of allowing for economic growth. The monetarists' prediction is, therefore, that the rate of inflation – the change in P – will be equal to the rate of growth of the money supply (M) two years ago, *less* the percentage rise in output.

Figure 17 compares the rate of growth of broad money with the rate of price inflation. The evidence of the graph is mixed. In the period to 1981, a rise in the supply of money appears to be related to a rise in the rate of inflation. The evidence in support of the monetarist case is strongest in the early 1970s when very high rates of growth in the money supply were followed by high inflation a few years later.

Inflation in the UK

Figure 17 Retail price inflation and broad money growth

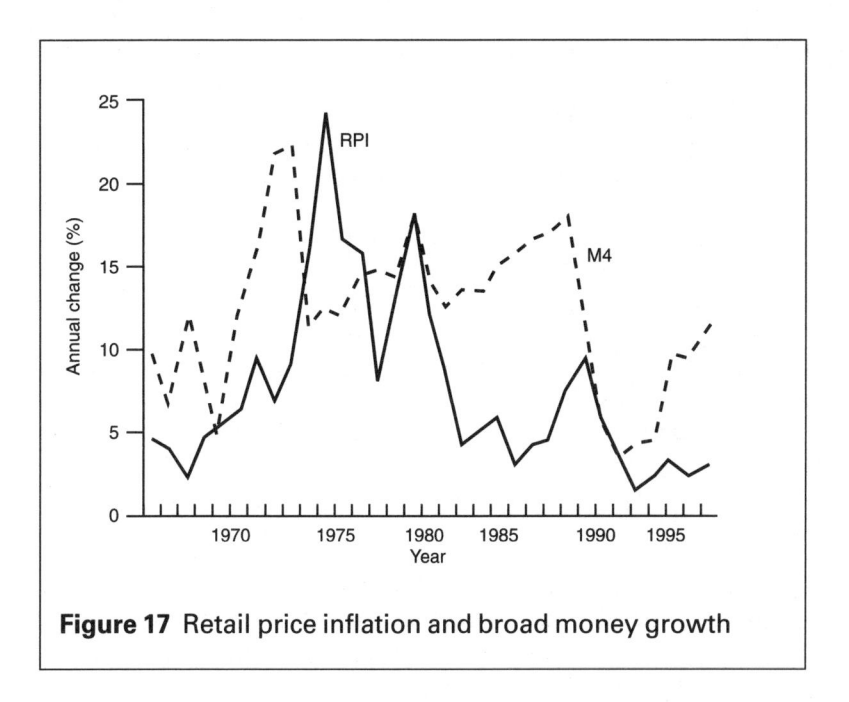

The time lag involved, however, appears to be highly variable. Let us take the period 1972 to 1974 as an example. 1972 saw a peak in the rate of broad money growth. According to monetarist theory this should have led to a peak in inflation two years later, but the peak occurred in 1975, not 1974. Later, in 1980, inflation and the growth of the money supply peaked together and thereafter the relationship appears to break down.

There appears to be some evidence of a link between the rate of growth of the money supply and inflation until 1981, but not in the exact way suggested by the monetarists. Further investigation is called for.

Perhaps the measure of the money supply we have used is wrong. There is, of course, more than one measure of the money supply and the quantity theory gives no indication of which would offer us the best guide to inflation. In fact in recent years the favoured measure of the money supply has changed several times and several measures once reported have been abandoned and replaced with new ones.

Figure 17 uses the broad money measure M4 which includes money held in bank and building society accounts. An alternative measure is M0, which is a narrow definition of the money supply dominated by notes and coins (see Chapter 6 for a fuller definition). Figure 18 shows

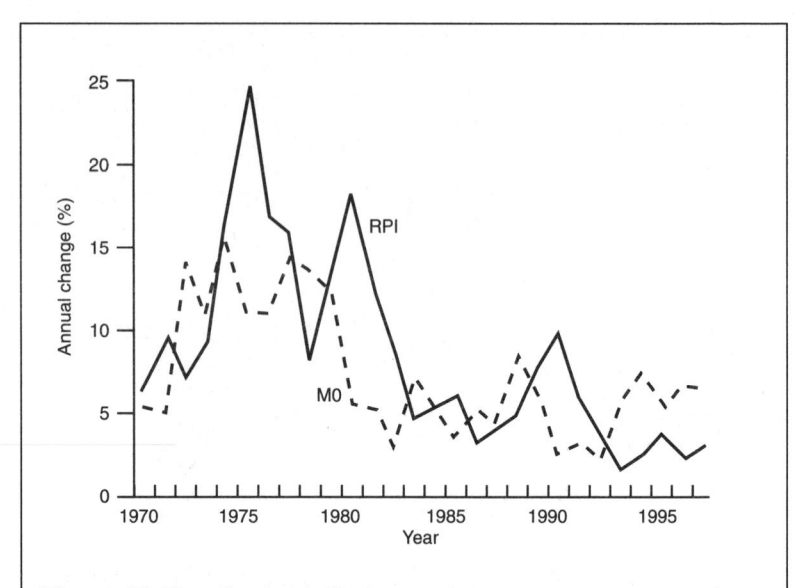

Figure 18 Retail price inflation and narrow money growth

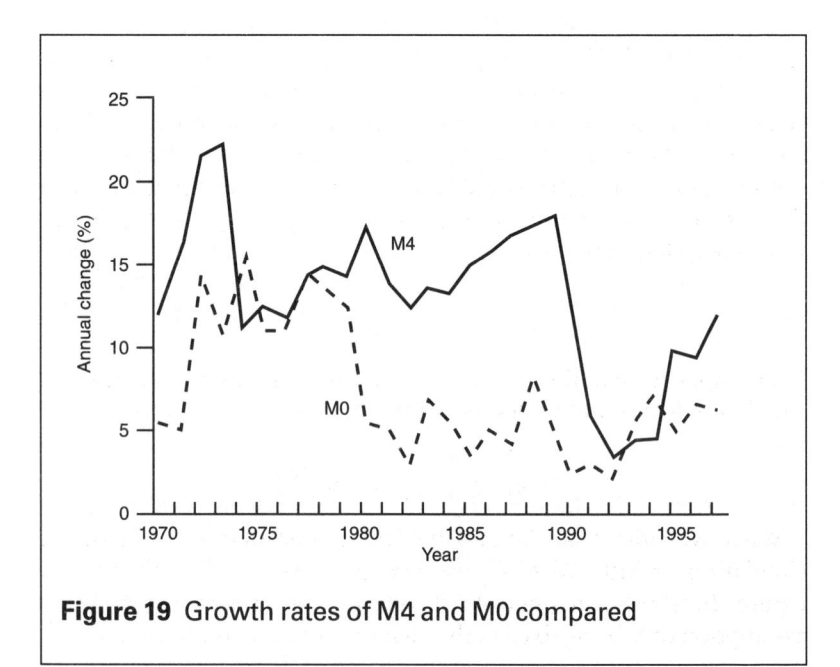

Figure 19 Growth rates of M4 and M0 compared

the relationship between M0 and retail price inflation. M0 seems to predict inflation rather better in the 1980s, but the relationship still breaks down in the 1990s.

A key point is that the relationship between the different measures of the money supply have broken down, as Figure 19 shows. The different measures of the money supply have behaved in such different ways in recent years that the prediction of inflation each would provide from the quantity theory would be very different.

Figures 18 and 19 have not taken account of the change in output which must be allowed for when testing the monetarists' case against the data. The monetarists never claimed a precise time lag, and would argue that many other factors – such as changing exchange rates and government policy – would cloud the issue. Overall there appears to be a strong link between the figures reported for inflation and the money supply in the 1970s, and this had a major effect on the thinking of those who guided government policy in the 1980s.

These data show that the relationship proposed by the quantity theory between the money supply and inflation has broken down. Very large rises in the rate of growth of the money supply did not feed through into inflation.

- **Some possible explanations**

How could the money supply rise so fast and there be no matching rise in inflation? A key assumption of the monetarists' case is a stable velocity of circulation, but if this were not the case then the strict relationship between the money supply and the price level is broken.

If the money supply rises and there is to be no rise in inflation, then the velocity of circulation must fall. For example, suppose the money supply doubles. At first we have:

$$M \times V = P \times Y$$
$$£1000 \times 5 = £1 \times 5000.$$

Now suppose that the money supply doubles but the velocity of circulation halves and the level of output remains at 5000 units:

$$M \times V = P \times Y$$
$$£2000 \times 2.5 = £1 \times 5000.$$

When we look at the data for the UK we find that the velocities of circulation of M0 and M4 have changed very significantly and, as Figure 20 shows, in opposite directions – so suggesting that the assumption of V being fixed in the quantity equation is not valid.

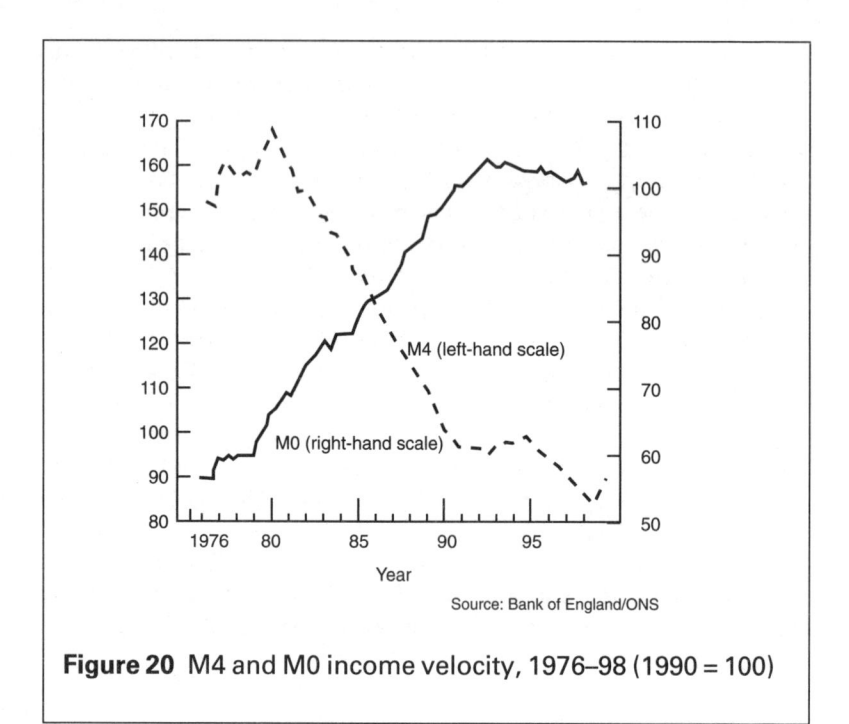

Figure 20 M4 and M0 income velocity, 1976–98 (1990 = 100)

There are, of course, reasons for this change in behaviour. There were significant changes in the working of the financial markets in the 1980s which led to important changes in behaviour and impacted on the rate of inflation.

- Deregulation of the financial markets and the removal of credit controls meant that households and firms were able to borrow more easily. Borrowing leads to higher money holdings in bank accounts, impacting directly on the M4 measure.
- The introduction and increasing availability of automatic cash machines and 'Switch' cards have made it easier to obtain cash, and this explains the rise in M0 velocity.

Whatever the true reasons, it is clear that the relationship described by the quantity theory of money has not explained inflation in the UK in recent years.

Movements of the aggregate price level and real output

In Chapter 4 we used the aggregate demand and supply model to illustrate alternative theories of the causes of inflation. Recall that this classified inflation as either demand-pull or cost-push. In the case of demand-pull inflation there was an initial movement of the aggregate demand curve to the right; and in the case of cost-push inflation the first movement was of the short-run aggregate supply curve to the left. Figure 21 maps the price level in the UK against the level of real GDP for the period 1975 to 1998.

The data in Figure 21 show what appears to be clear evidence of movements of the aggregate demand curve to the right, implying that inflation in the UK has been mainly of the demand-pull variety. The movement of aggregate demand to the right in the mid-to-late 1980s shows the effect of the consumer boom of that period quite clearly. It is not always possible to be absolutely sure about the cause of inflation, because of wage–price spirals. For example the apparent shift to the right of aggregate demand from 1975 to 1979 might be a response to a shift to the left of the aggregate supply curve in previous years. Nor is it always possible to say if the cause of the shift of the aggregate demand curve was due to excessive monetary growth or to a rise in aggregate demand. *Each case deserves individual investigation.*

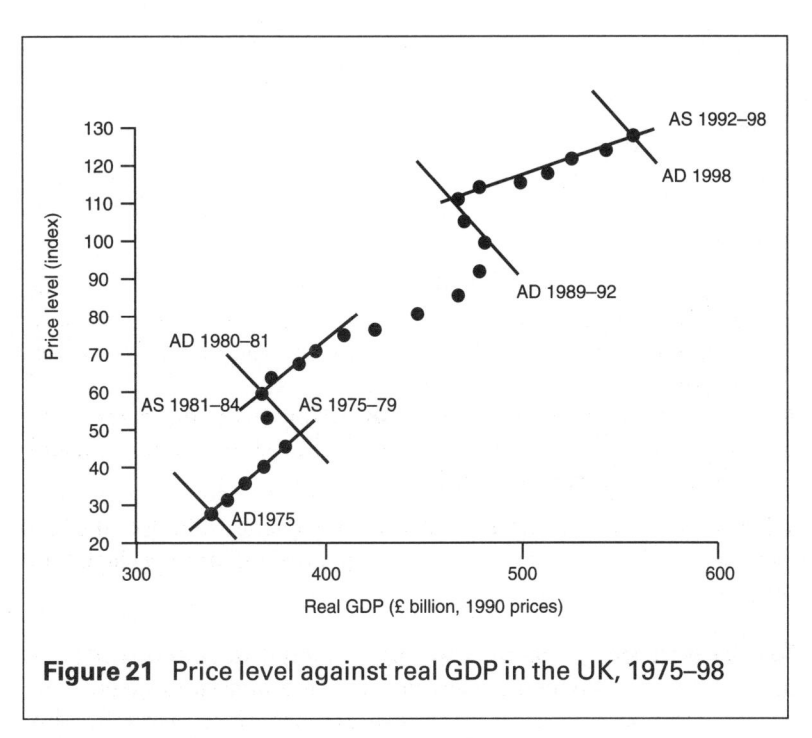

Figure 21 Price level against real GDP in the UK, 1975–98

The movement of the aggregate supply curve between 1979 and 1981 gives some support to the idea of cost-push inflation. This was a period of rising oil prices. However, there is little to support the idea of continuing independent cost-push inflation in the UK. The adjustment of the supply curve in the periods 1979–81 and 1989–92 is exactly what we would expect following a movement of the aggregate demand curve to the right. The period since 1992 shows a sustained movement of the aggregate demand curve to the right.

Summing up

It would appear that neither the Keynesian nor the monetarists' explanations of inflation can entirely explain recent experience in the UK. This may be rather frustrating for students, because there is apparently no conclusion to be drawn and the controversy continues. In itself this is a problem for policymakers who need to understand the cause of inflation if they are to be able to form a policy to control it. The ever-changing nature of the economy means that past experience may be only a rough guide to the future. Evidently we are *not* all Keynesians now.

KEY WORDS

Stagflation	Natural rate of employment
Real wages	Natural rate of unemployment
Expectations-augmented Phillips curves	Long-run Phillips curve
	NAIRU

Further reading

Atkinson, B., Livesey, F. and Milward., R., Chapter 22 in *Applied Economics*, Macmillan, 1998

Bootle, R., Chapters 7 and 8 in *The Death of Inflation*, Nicholas Brealey, 1996.

Griffiths, A. and Wall, S. (eds), Chapter 19 in *Applied Economics*, Addison-Wesley Longman, 1997.

Smith, D., Chapter 4 in *UK Current Economic Policy*, Heinemann Educational, 1999.

Useful website

For access to worldwide data and links: www.globalfindata.com

Essay questions
1. (a) Explain the Phillips curve. [10 marks]
   (b) Discuss whether the Phillips curve is 'dead'. [15 marks]
2. (a) Explain the Fisher equation. [10marks]
   (b) Discuss whether the Fisher equation provides an adequate explanation of inflation. [15 marks]

Data response question
This task is based on a question set by the University of Oxford Delegacy of Local Examinations in 1998. Study Table A and then answer the questions that follow, using your knowledge of economics and economic analysis.

Table A Unemployment and inflation in the UK

Year	UK unemployment rate (%)	UK retail prices annual change (inflation) (%)
1988	8.1	4.9
1989	6.3	7.8
1990	5.9	9.5
1991	8.1	5.9
1992	9.9	3.7
1993	10.4	1.6
1994	9.3	2.5
1995	8.3	3.4

Source: *National Institute Economic Review*, October 1996.

1. From your studies, and using the data in Table A, discuss the relationship between unemployment and inflation. [14 marks]
2. Discuss which objective, high employment or low inflation, is receiving greatest priority from the government. [6 marks]

Chapter Six
The basis of monetary policy

'The overriding objective of monetary policy is price stability.'
Eddie George, Governor of the Bank of England, November 1992

Monetary policy can be either:

- the manipulation of the money supply by the government, or
- the manipulation of the rate of interest by the government.

The purpose of this policy may be to:

- influence the level of economic activity, or
- influence the exchange rate, or
- directly control inflation.

At various times in the UK all of the above have been applied.

Monetary policy is just one possible economic policy at the disposal of the government. The other main macroeconomic policy tool to influence the economy in the short and medium term is fiscal policy. Fiscal policy is the regulation of government spending and taxation and most changes to this are announced each year in the budget by the Chancellor of the Exchequer. Other policies available are supply-side policies and regulation, both of which are microeconomic policies.

Monetary policy must operate in conjunction with the financial markets, which are made up of numerous independent banks and institutional and personal investors. The Central Bank has the key role in the operation of monetary policy, and we will examine both the financial markets and the role of the Bank of England before looking at the theory of how monetary policy operates.

Financial markets

The function of the financial markets is to channel funds from those who have a surplus and who wish to make a profit on their use, to those who require funds and are prepared to pay for them. The wide range of people and firms lending and borrowing funds leads to a diversity of financial institutions, each of which caters for a certain sector of the financial market.

We can identify a number of types of institution which make up the financial markets.

The basis of monetary policy

- **Commercial banks,** such as Lloyds/TSB and National Westminster, accept deposits from the public and firms and make loans to them. They are responsible for a large proportion of credit creation.
- **Merchant banks** advise firms in takeovers and new share floatations and act as their agents.
- **Building societies** now act more like commercial banks in that they can provide cheque accounts and lend for more purposes than just home purchase.
- **Insurance companies** accept premiums in return for taking a risk, and **pension funds** invest money to provide income for retired workers. Both build up large reserves which they invest in a wide range of assets.
- **Stock exchanges** exist to bring together potential investors and firms seeking funds. Firms can offer shares for sale on the exchange, and those with funds to invest can buy them, receiving in return dividends from profits and capital gains as the share price rises.

The financial markets are, therefore, a vital part of the economy. Any failure of these markets would seriously damage the economy's ability to operate.

The role and function of the central bank

There are a number of important functions of the Bank of England that allow it to conduct monetary policy more effectively.

- *The issuing of notes and coins.* This allows the Bank of England to control the amount of cash in the financial system if it wishes.
- *Acting as the bankers' bank.* Each commercial bank maintains an account at the Bank of England, so this set-up can be used to control lending policy.
- *Acting as lender of last resort.* The Bank of England will always ensure that banks have the necessary liquidity to meet their obligations to customers; however, the price (rate of interest) they charge can be used for policy purposes.
- *Issuing and managing government debt.* The Bank of England raises any new loans the government requires and manages the outstanding debt. It is also for the Bank of England to influence market interest rates by the prices it accepts, or refuses to accept, for the sale of new bills and bonds.

This combination of roles allows the Bank of England significant influence within the financial markets, and so the ability to conduct monetary policy, without the need for legislation as is often required for fiscal policy. The ability to alter monetary policy in this way allows greater flexibility to the government, although monetary policy typically takes some time to influence the economy.

The importance of bank deposits in the money supply

It is generally believed that the source of the money supply is the Bank of England and the Royal Mint. In fact the bulk of the money supply in the UK is made up of deposits in commercial banks and building society cheque accounts (we shall refer to all these institutions as the 'banks').

The extent to which money in bank deposits dominates the money supply is shown by the fact that, for December 1998, the following figures were reported:

$$M0: \quad £29\,095$$
$$M4: \quad £782\,535$$

- M0 is defined as notes and coins in circulation, plus money in banks' tills plus bankers' operational deposits at the Bank of England.
- M4 is defined as notes and coins in circulation, plus private sector sterling deposits (both interest-bearing and non-interest-bearing) in commercial banks and building societies, plus sterling certificates of deposit.

M0 is thus the narrowest definition of the money supply reported and is clearly in the control of the Bank of England. M4 is currently the widest definition of the money supply reported.

The difference between the two measures is almost entirely bank deposits and shows the importance of such deposits. One of the reasons why there is such a huge difference between the amount of 'cash' and the amount of 'money' is because banks are able to create money by making loans to customers.

The UK money supply defined

Just two measures of the money supply were used above to illustrate the importance of bank deposits to the money supply. These are the only measures of the money supply currently reported.

In contrast, in the past many more measures of the money supply were reported. The reason for having more than one measure of the money supply is to allow the statistics to encompass all the various functions money is asked to perform. At the most basic level, money must have two roles:

- it must act as a 'medium of exchange'
- it must act as a 'store of value'.

The role as a medium of exchange is fulfilled by cash and access to cheques, which, while they are not money themselves, are a claim on money. Cash allows transactions to take place in the market and can be described as the narrowest definition of money in the economy; hence M0 is known as a 'narrow' definition of the money supply or, in the terminology of the Bank of England, the **narrow monetary aggregate**.

The role as a store of value can be undertaken by many assets, not all of them acceptable as money because these assets are not generally acceptable in settlement of debt in general trading. There are many accounts classed as money that fulfil the store-of-value function and these are included in the M4 definition of money. M4 is known as the **broad monetary aggregate**.

The tendency of our definition of 'money' to change presents economists and politicians with enormous problems – particularly those seeking to prove or use a relationship between money supply and inflation. It is clear that bank deposits make up a significant part of M4, and so we shall now look at how the banking system can expand the money supply by making loans (extending credit).

Credit creation

Let us take the simple situation where there is just one bank in the economy. Let us further suppose that the bank, in accordance with the rules or good practice, always keeps a minimum of 10 per cent of its total liabilities in cash. This cash would be needed to meet the daily demands of depositors withdrawing money from their accounts. While there seems no reason for withdrawals to exceed deposits there is also no reason for the timings to match exactly.

If the Bank of England issues some new cash this passes into circulation and is spent on consumer or investment goods. The firms receiving this revenue place some of the money in the bank and this gives the bank extra cash in its tills. The money, of course, belongs to the customer (the bank is liable to repay it at any time), but the bank knows that it is never likely to be called upon for more than one-tenth of its total liabilities each day. The bank could then take 90 per cent of the newly deposited cash and lend it to another customer who requires a loan, and by charging interest on that loan make a profit.

This is not the bank's most profitable course, however. A better approach would be to keep all the cash in the bank and make a loan equal to nine times the size of the new cash deposit by simply crediting the accounts of borrowers. The bank has simply created the money it has lent to customers by writing it into their accounts and honouring all cheques and demands for cash withdrawals. The bank has maintained the required ratio of cash to liabilities at 1:10 (the customers' original deposits plus nine times the deposit as loans to other customers) and so will be able to meet all calls for cash.

The ability of banks to create money in this way depends on the proportion of cash, or very liquid assets, they need to keep as a proportion of their total liabilities. If the proportion is 10 per cent, deposits can rise by 1/0.1, or ten times the original deposits. The banks can create loans, and hence money, up to an amount equal to the rise in deposits minus the original deposit. This is known as the **credit multiplier**. If the banks need keep only 5 per cent of their liabilities in cash, then the credit multiplier is 1/0.05 or 20.

The significance of the credit multiplier

The description of the banking system in the last section is simplistic. Banks need to keep a range of interest-earning assets that are easily converted into cash – **liquid assets** – in order to allow them to operate freely. They may, for example, keep a *liquidity ratio* (liquid assets to total assets) of 15 per cent. Banks are also required to maintain a *capital adequacy ratio* (bank's capital to total assets) and of course operate in a system with many other banks. None of this invalidates the essential point that banks, given an expanding cash base, can create a great deal of money in the form of bank deposits.

From this analysis it should be clear that if a government wishes to operate a monetary policy it must be able to control, or at least influence, the ability of banks to create money.

The aim of monetary policy

Today, under the influence of the monetarists, the aim of monetary policy is generally agreed to be the control of inflation, as stated explicitly by the Bank of England. Previously, under the influence of the Keynesians, the aim of monetary policy was to influence the level of aggregate demand. These two periods cannot be precisely separated.

- During the earlier period of demand management, typically direct controls of the money supply were employed.
- During the later period, inflation has been the target and more indirect methods have been used, usually working through the demand for credit by controlling interest rates.

Influencing the *supply of money* directly

The aim of influencing the money supply directly was to affect the level of aggregate demand.

Figure 22 shows the effect of reducing the money supply in the **money market**. The money market is where banks and other financial institutions and large companies lend or borrow money. The sums involved are considerable and all transactions are settled on the same day. The fall in the money supply from MS_1 to MS_2 (in the top part of the diagram) leads to a new equilibrium in the money market, and the rate of interest rises from r_1 to r_2. The rise in the rate of interest – which is the price of borrowing money – leads to a fall in the level of planned investment, as given by the investment demand schedule, from I_1 to I_2.

Investment (I) is one component of aggregate demand, and a highly influential one. The fall in investment from I_1 to I_2 causes a fall in aggregate demand. The aggregate demand curve thus shifts from AD_1 to AD_2 (in the bottom part of the diagram). Notice that although the aim of the policy may have been to reduce aggregate demand, and so

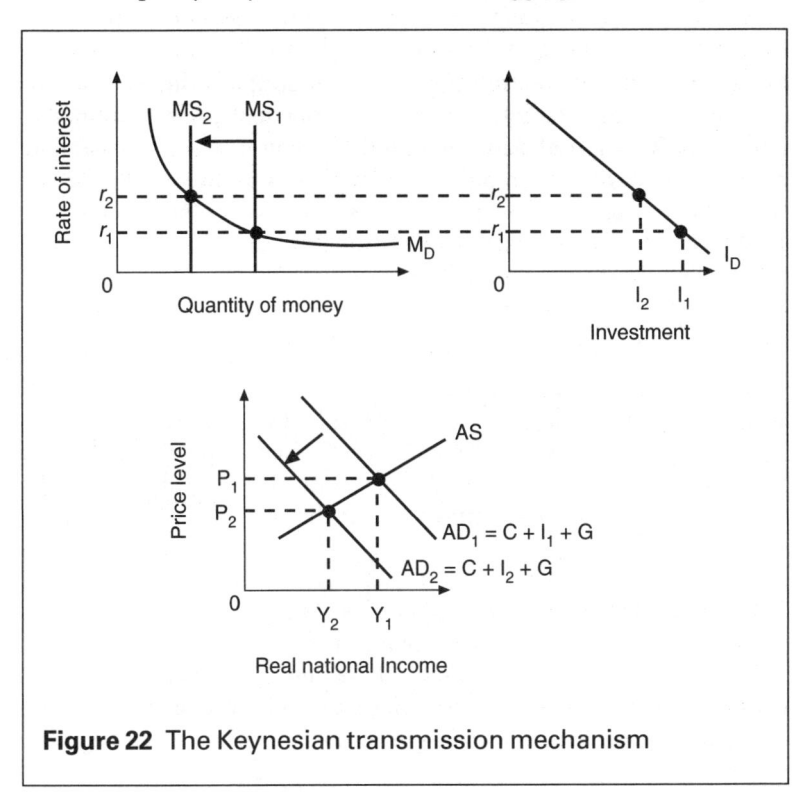

Figure 22 The Keynesian transmission mechanism

reduce real national income, it also may affect the price level, which falls from P_1 to P_2 – but this will depend on the slope of the aggregate supply curve, AS.

This view of how changes in the money supply affect real output and the price level is a description of what is known as the **transmission mechanism** between the monetary and real sectors of the economy. The transmission mechanism shown in Figure 22 is the *Keynesian transmission mechanism*, which results in a lower level of output and a lower price level. The *monetarist view*, as outlined in Chapter 4, would suggest that the transmission mechanism between the money market and the price level is as outlined in the quantity theory of money. The fall in the money supply from MS_1 to MS_2 would, therefore, reduce the price level and in the longer term leave real output unchanged at the natural rate.

Both monetarists and Keynesians can agree on some of the effects of a rise or fall in the money supply, but not on how the effects come about. They also disagree on the extent of the effect the change in the money supply would have, and we shall look at this again later.

- **Techniques for controlling the money supply directly**

The Bank of England had a number of possible tools of monetary control at its disposal during the period when it was felt feasible to attempt to control the money supply. Each was used with varying degrees of success. The first two methods discussed below relied on the existence of legally enforced reserve ratios and aimed at making use of the principle of the *credit multiplier*.

Open market operations

The Bank of England could influence the cash reserves of the commercial banks directly through the buying or selling of **government securities** to the public, such as consols and other long-term bonds.

Suppose the Bank wished to reduce the money supply. It would offer for sale government long-term securities to the general public, who would purchase them by writing cheques that would be drawn against their bank accounts. The Bank of England would present the cheques for payment to the purchasers' banks, which would settle the debts from balances they held in their accounts with the Bank of England. As these balances at the Bank of England form part of the commercial banks' cash reserves, a policy of selling government securities effectively reduces those reserves, causing a multiple contraction of the broad money supply. Purchasing government securities from the public has the reverse effect.

Special deposits

A far more direct approach to reducing the money supply would be to take away cash reserves from the commercial banks, so forcing a multiple contraction of the money supply as they reduced their liabilities. This was the intention of **special deposits**.

The Bank of England could simply call on the commercial banks to deposit part of their reserve assets with them, and banks were not permitted to sell long-term securities to finance these deposits. Once deposited, these balances (whilst still belonging to the commercial banks) could not be counted as part of the banks' cash or reserve assets. Special deposits then restricted further profitable lending.

Quantitative controls

This method of control was used in the mid-1970s, when banks were told to limit their expansion to a certain percentage over each specified period. Exceeding the maximum permitted rate of growth meant that a bank was required to place a percentage of the excess in a special deposit (a **supplementary special deposit**). The penalties were on a sliding scale: the more the permitted growth rate was exceeded, the higher the proportion of the excess growth that had to be deposited. The larger the banks became, the more the controls squeezed them – hence the system became known as 'the corset'!

Monetary base control

The monetarist school of thought suggests that controlling the money supply is crucial to the control of inflation.

The monetarist policy prescription is that the government should adopt a 'monetary rule' – and stick to it. A suitable monetary rule might be *'the money supply will be limited to a growth rate of 4 per cent a year'*. If the trend growth rate of the economy is 2 per cent a year, and if the rule is implemented, according to the quantity theory of money inflation should average around 2 per cent over the medium to long term. This is not a policy that has ever been tried in the UK, but a number of suggestions have been put forward as to how it might operate, the best known of which is **monetary base control**.

The idea is to control the supply of **'high-powered money'** that forms the basis of the financial system's liquidity; this is mainly cash in circulation. If the amount of cash is restricted, then so is the liquidity of the banking system, and so will be the ability of the banks to create credit. As the supply of cash is directly in the control of the government, the implementation of the policy should be achievable.

The principal objection to monetary base control is that interest rates would become volatile as attempts were made to keep the level of high-powered money within the required range. This would be destabilizing for the whole economy.

Influencing the *demand for money*

In Figure 22 we saw that influencing the money supply led to a new equilibrium in the money markets. If it is accepted that the money markets clear quickly, a change in the demand for money would also lead to a new equilibrium.

The demand for money depends upon a number of factors, such as incomes, the base rate of interest, and expectations about changes in these and other variables. The monetarists contend that the demand for money is a stable function of the rate of interest and point to historical data to support their view. Figure 23 shows the relationship between the rate of interest and the demand for money. The horizontal axis is the ratio of money to GDP – this is used because the demand for money depends on the number of transactions (measured by output). Thus the graph shows how the quantity of money *per transaction* changes as the rate of interest changes.

The relationship shown in Figure 23 was found to be remarkably stable for the UK in the long period 1920 to 1983. Thus the monetarists

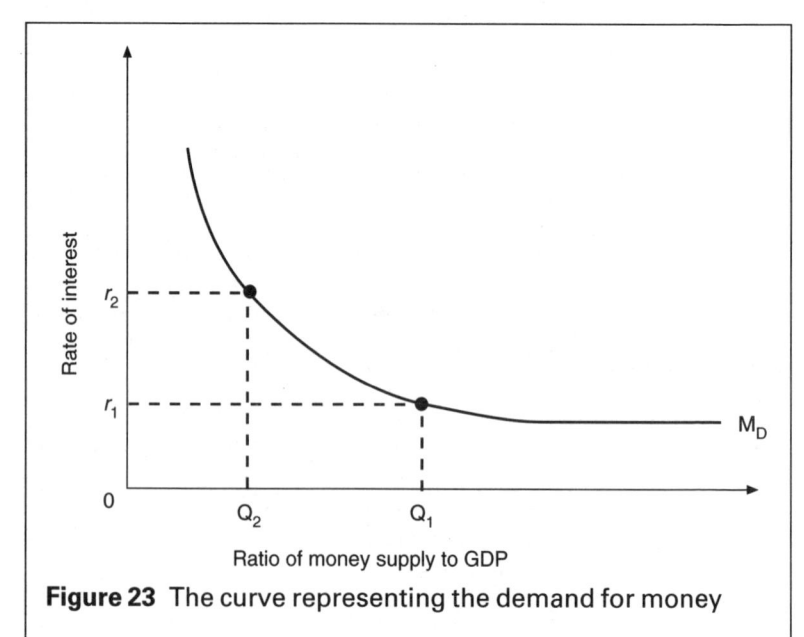

Figure 23 The curve representing the demand for money

argued in favour of simply changing the rate of interest to cause a movement along the money demand function (M_D), and allowing the money market to clear at this new rate of interest.

Raising the rate of interest, it was argued – say from r_1 to r_2 in Figure 23 – would raise the cost of borrowing and so reduce the demand for new loans. Banks would not be able to expand the money supply by extending as much credit as before, and so this would lead to a lower money supply – or more accurately a slower growth in the money supply – and be an effective anti-inflation policy.

A crucial matter in this theory is the stability of the curve representing the demand for money. The demand-for-money function was very stable until 1973, but deviated from past observations in 1974/75, and finally showed instability from the late 1980s. If, when interest rates are changed, the money demand curve shifts, then the outcome is uncertain. For example, raising interest rates in Figure 23 could lead to the money demand curve shifting to the right, leading to no fall in money demand at all.

- Control of interest rates

To be able to implement monetary policy via the demand side of the money markets, it is necessary to be able to influence the rate of interest. This is certainly something governments claim they are able to do, but things are rather more complicated than they appear.

Often the news carries the headline:

BANK OF ENGLAND RAISES INTEREST RATES

This implies that the Bank can simply announce the rate of interest to be applied in the markets, which is not correct. The Bank must also take action to ensure that the rate of interest really does move in the markets.

The Bank has used the rate at which it will discount bills to the commercial banks as a way of influencing the short-term interest rates. Often called **base rate**, this represents the official rate at which banks can obtain cash from the Bank of England.

However, this is just *one* interest rate paid on one type of asset; there are many assets each with its own interest rate. These rates do, nevertheless, tend to move up and down in unison, so by raising the base rate the Bank of England *can* influence all other rates in the financial markets.

There are several other ways of influencing interest rates, all of which are based on keeping the banking system short of cash so that it must regularly obtain funds from the Bank of England. The Bank of England can reduce *liquidity* in the system by selling long-term securities in the market. This rise in the supply of long-term securities causes the price of securities to fall, raising the rate of interest paid on them.

The Bank can also restructure the national debt, moving the balance of debt away from the more liquid short-term bills and issuing a greater proportion of long-term bills. This can be done quite easily because Treasury bills have a life of only 90 days. When they are due for repayment, fewer Treasury bills and more long-term securities can be issued in order to repay the holders, leaving the financial institutions with fewer liquid assets and again causing institutions to offer a higher rate of interest to obtain the use of the liquid assets they need.

A third alternative is simply to issue more government debt when the Bank of England wants to raise interest rates. The rise in supply of government debt will cause the price of government securities to fall, and this implies a rise in the rate of interest paid on those securities.

Exactly how the Bank of England influences short term interest rates is discussed in Chapter 8.

- The effects of changing interest rates

Interest rates affect the economy by moving the aggregate demand curve. This can come about in a number of ways. Let us take the effect of a rise in interest rates as an example:

- Spending decisions are affected, as saving now will yield a higher rate of return. At the same time, borrowing becomes less attractive.

THE PRICE OF BONDS AND THE INTEREST RATE

The price of a bond is inversely related to the rate of interest. For example, consider a security that pays £10 a year to the owner. Ignoring the possibility of the security being redeemed (repaid), if the market rate of interest is 10 per cent then someone would be prepared to pay up to £100 to buy the security. £10 is 10 per cent of £100 and so represents a rate of return to the holder at least as good as they could get elsewhere in the markets. If the rate of interest were 20 per cent then someone would be prepared to pay up to £50 to obtain an annual interest payment of £10, being 20 per cent of the purchase price. *Hence when the interest rate goes up the price of securities falls.* As all other financial assets will need to offer a competitive rate of interest, their prices will also need to fall. Hence all interest rates in the economy will follow.

The basis of monetary policy

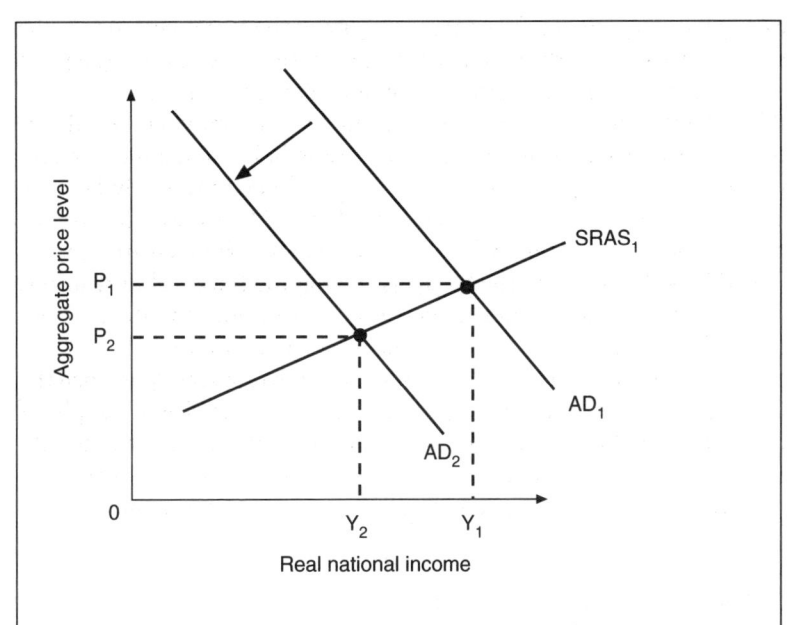

Figure 24 The effect on aggregate demand of raising interest rates

Households will be induced to delay some spending now in favour of more saving and less borrowing. Firms will also be induced to delay investments.
- Borrowers and lenders find that their cash-flow positions are affected. Borrowers with variable-interest loans are asked to make higher repayments (usually each month) – this especially affects households with mortgages (see Chapter 9). Lenders will find they receive higher payments. These changes in cash flow may affect spending.
- A rise in interest rates will affect the value of certain assets. House prices, bonds and shares are good examples. House prices may fall as the cost of a mortgage rises; bond prices will fall as the return they offer becomes less competitive; and shares may react in either direction depending on the prevailing opinion on the effect of the interest rate rise. Those who hold assets that have fallen in value will feel worse off and this may reduce spending.
- Import prices influence inflation. If interest rates in the UK rise, the relatively higher returns available in sterling assets will attract an inflow of capital and lead to an appreciation of the exchange rate. A

Instrument	Intermediate variables	Target
Rate of interest ➡	Demand for money Money supply ➡	Inflation

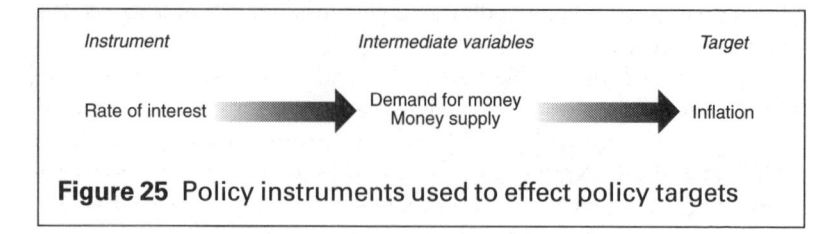

Figure 25 Policy instruments used to effect policy targets

rising pound reduces import prices and raises export prices. Demand for UK produced goods falls.

The effect of raising interest rates is shown in Figure 24, the aggregate demand curve shifting to the left. A fall in interest rates has the reverse effect.

Time lags in the effects of policy

No economic policy has immediately the full effect that the policymaker intended; *all economic policies operate with a lag*. It is possible to identify two types, the **inside lag** and the **outside lag**.

- The inside lag

This is the time taken for the authorities to implement a policy. There are often delays in data collection and in recognizing that there has been a permanent change in the direction of a variable – such as inflation. Once policymakers have decided that action must be taken there is a further delay while the policy is implemented.

The inside lag for monetary policy is typically much shorter than the inside lag for fiscal policy. Changes in direct taxes and expenditure are announced annually in the budget and indirect taxes can be altered only by 10 per cent between budgets without Parliament's permission. Monetary policy changes can be made quite quickly, the Bank of England acting as soon as the decision is made.

- The outside lag

This is the time taken to influence the targeted variables – i.e. the time the policy measures take to work through the economy.

It is helpful at this point to distinguish between instruments, intermediate targets and targets. An **instrument** is the variable over which the government has control and which it changes in order to effect a policy change. Usually the policy instrument (say the rate of interest) does not affect the policy **target** directly (say inflation), but works by affecting other **intermediate variables** (intermediate targets) which do impact directly upon the target variable. A simple example is shown in Figure 25.

The length of time of the outside lag will depend on many factors, such as when the policy is implemented, other policy measures enacted, and so on. The difficulty of identifying turning points in economic variables and the length of time policy takes to affect the economy has led many, particularly monetarists, to suggest that *precise control of the economy, known as fine tuning, is impossible.*

KEY WORDS

Commercial banks	Government securities
Merchant banks	Special deposits
Building societies	Quantitative controls
Insurance companies	Supplementary special deposit
Pension funds	Monetary base control
Stock exchanges	High-powered money
Central bank	Base rate
Narrow monetary aggregate	Inside lag
Broad monetary aggregate	Outside lag
Credit multiplier	Instrument
Liquid assets	Target
Money markets	Intermediate variables
Transmission mechanism	

Further reading

Anderton, A., Units 91 and 95 in *Economics*, 2nd edn, Causeway Press, 1995.

Grant, S., Chapter 61 in *Stanlake's Introductory Economics*, Longman, 1999.

Maunder, P. *et al.*, Chapter 28 in *Economics Explained*, 3rd edn, Collins Educational, 1995.

Sloman, J., Chapters 18 and 19 in *Economics*, 3rd edn, Prentice Hall, 1997.

Useful website

Financial Times, www.ft.com/hippocampus/

Essay questions
1. (a) How does the Bank of England attempt to influence interest rates? [12 marks]
   (b) Discuss the role of monetary policy in controlling inflation. [13 marks] [Associated Examining Board 1998]
2. The rate of inflation in France was reported to have been 8 per cent in 1996.
   (a) Explain what this figure means and how it might have been calculated. [8 marks]
   (b) Analyse the policies that a government might adopt in order to reduce the rate of inflation, and comment upon the likely conflicts which might be involved. [12 marks] [OCR, The National Economy, 1997]

Data response question
This task is based on a question set by the University of Oxford Delegacy of Local Examinations in 1997. Read the piece below and study Table A. Then answer the questions that follow.

In the UK, despite rises in raw-material and import prices, plus higher indirect taxation, retail prices in general have barely moved. Why? The obvious answer is, of course, the effect of the recession on consumer spending, together with the flood of 'special offers' and discounts that have become available.

Another way of looking at it is to suppose that business can opt for either a 'high-price, low-output' or 'low-price, high-output' strategy. In many sectors there is an understanding that the second strategy is the more profitable. Customers are now acutely price-sensitive, as they were not when inflation was high and companies could become complacent and inefficient. It is generally held that low price inflation benefits the consumer and the economy in general.

But is this necessarily the case? One way of keeping prices low is to be ruthless in keeping costs down, and this may mean shedding labour as well as keeping wages low. Moreover, firms are more likely to expand by means of horizontal mergers, which may bring about economies of scale, than by taking the risk of introducing new products. Such policies may hold down household real incomes and increase monopoly power.

Yet a look at the success of economies such as Germany and Japan indicates that it is possible to combine low inflation with growth and high employment. The problem for the UK is how to do this too.

The basis of monetary policy

Table A International economic performance (percentage figures)

Country	Growth rate [a]	Growth per head [b]	Inflation [c]	Unemployment [d]
Japan	4.3	3.6	1.5	2.5
Spain	3.2	2.9	8.7	22.7
USA	3.1	1.7	3.9	6.7
UK	2.8	2.4	5.7	10.2
Italy	2.4	2.2	9.1	11.5
Germany	2.3	2.4	2.7	8.2
France	2.3	1.7	5.4	11.6
Netherlands	2.1	1.6	1.7	7.5
OECD average	2.6	1.6	5.0	8.1

[a] Annual growth rate of GNP, 1980–91
[b] Annual average growth rate of GNP per head, 1980–92
[c] Average annual growth of inflation, 1980–92
[d] Unemployment rate, 1993
Source: *Human Development Report* 1995.

1. (a) What is meant by the phrase 'customers are now acutely price sensitive'? [4 marks]
   (b) Give *two* explanations why consumer sensitivity to price appears to have increased in the UK. [4 marks]
2. Explain in what type of market businesses may have a choice of a 'high-price, low-output' or 'low-price, high-output' strategy. [16 marks]
3. (a) Explain why 'It is generally held that low price inflation benefits the consumer and the economy in general'. [16 marks]
   (b) To what extent do the data provide support for the view that a low-inflation environment is an important ingredient of successful economic performance? [22 marks]
4. Compare the effectiveness of lowering interest rates or increasing government expenditure as methods of achieving both low inflation and high employment. [18 marks]

Chapter Seven
Implementing monetary policy

'*The acid test of monetary policy is its record in reducing inflation. ...
The inflation rate is judge and jury.*'
Nigel Lawson when Chancellor of the Exchequer

The changing role of monetary policy
Monetary policy is just one component of overall economic policy. Over the last 30 years the opinion of policymakers has changed significantly and often as to what role monetary policy should play in general macroeconomic policy.

In this chapter we shall be looking at how monetary policy has been operated in various ways up to 1997. The operation of policy does not always conform to the theory we have discussed in earlier chapters of this book, and so we shall trace out the frequent changes in policy and try to explain why they came about. An understanding of monetary policy relies to some extent on understanding its history.

The Keynesian era of monetary policy
We have already seen that the Keynesian explanation of inflation rested on there being too much aggregate demand in the presence of certain bottlenecks in supply. If the control of aggregate demand, via fiscal policy, went beyond the full-employment level, then there would be an inflationary gap, and prices, rather than employment, would begin to increase.

The view of Keynesians was that monetary policy was of little use. If there was a rise in the money supply Keynesians believed that any excess would simply be absorbed into idle balances and not affect the real economy. The standard opinion was that changes in the money supply did not matter very much.

If monetary policy was used for domestic purposes then it was used to support fiscal policy in an attempt to influence aggregate demand. In fact monetary policy was unavailable for most of the period between 1947 and 1971 because the UK operated within a fixed exchange-rate system. The **Bretton Woods system**, as it was known, required the government to keep the value of the pound sterling within certain narrowly defined limits relative to the US dollar. If there was downward pressure on the pound owing to increased sales of sterling (say because of a current account deficit), the Bank of England had to buy pounds with foreign currency reserves in order to equate demand and supply at the agreed exchange rate.

The net effect of this was that the domestic money supply was decreased. *In this way money and monetary policy were constrained to maintaining the exchange rate and could not be used for domestic policy concerns.* This situation arose again during the UK's membership of the European Union's fixed exchange-rate regime, the ERM, between 1990 and 1992.

Anti-inflation policy in the Keynesian era

The discussion of direct controls of the money supply in Chapter 6 was mainly concerned with pre-1971 theory. Anti-inflation policy was carried out by reducing aggregate demand through fiscal measures when an inflationary gap arose. There were two other anti-inflation policies employed in the period, although strictly neither comes under the heading of monetary policy – these were **prices and incomes policies** and **credit controls**.

- Prices and incomes policies

These were implemented intermittently throughout the period 1947 to 1978. The basis of such policies was the Phillips curve (see Figure 15 on page 49). Given this 'trade-off' between inflation and unemployment, it was up to the politicians to decide what combination of inflation and unemployment they preferred; they then operated on aggregate demand until they reached their preferred point on the Phillips curve. If the government chose high inflation and low unemployment, then consumers and exporters complained. If they chose low inflation and high unemployment, then trade unions complained.

Through prices and incomes policies the government tried to change the shape of the Phillips curve. The government tried to persuade workers not to take advantage of labour shortages by pushing up wages, and to persuade producers not to take advantage of excess demand for their goods by putting up prices.

This formed the basis of the various prices and incomes policies called the **Social Contract** by the then Prime Minister, Harold Wilson. The 'contract', between the government and labour on the one hand and between the government and producers on the other hand, was that the government would increase aggregate demand so as to keep unemployment down to very low levels provided that no-one took advantage of the high level of demand to increase wages or prices. Voluntary or statutory guidelines on wage increases were issued, and if these were observed it would be possible to move the Phillips curve to a lower level of inflation at each level of unemployment.

Prices and incomes policies were, however, ineffective and may be summed up as follows:

> '... whilst some incomes policies have reduced the rate of wage inflation during the period in which they operated, this reduction has only been temporary. Wage increases in the period immediately following the ending of policies were higher ... and these increases match losses incurred during the operation of the incomes policy.'

Henry and Ormerod, *National Institute Economic Review*, August 1978

- Credit controls

Throughout the Keynesian period the dominant theory put almost all the emphasis on controlling aggregate demand through fiscal policy. But some attention was paid to controlling credit. Typically this control was exercised on the credit which households used for buying consumer durables. The controls were of two forms, the so-called 'down-payment' and the period of repayment.

To borrow £100 it was necessary to already have, say, £10 or £30 to pay towards the good. To restrict credit, the minimum amount required, as a percentage of value, could be raised – restricting the number of households that could now afford to obtain credit. Shortening the repayment period made each repayment higher and so again reduced the ability of households to take up credit.

Credit controls were aimed at restricting aggregate demand, but acted on credit. Today the credit markets are international, *making such controls impracticable.*

The era of 'money matters' and 'inflation first'

It is difficult to separate the Keynesian era from the period when monetarism first became the primary influence behind UK government policy. In 1976 the then Labour government did introduce targets for the money supply and pursued policies that had as their aim the reduction of inflation at the expense of job losses. On the election of Mrs Thatcher and the Conservative government in 1979, the top priority of policy had definitely switched away from unemployment to the control of inflation.

The Chancellor of the Exchequer in the first Thatcher administration, Sir Geoffrey Howe, spelt out monetarist policy in a budget statement in 1979:

> *'We are committed to the progressive reduction of the rate of growth of the money supply.'*

This was followed one year later by the advent of the **medium-term financial strategy** (MTFS) which set targets for money supply and **the public sector borrowing requirement** (PSBR) from 1980 to 1984. Annual increases in money supply were to be reduced from between 7 and 11 per cent to between 4 and 8 per cent over that period. This pre-commitment of a four-year programme of slowing down the rate of change of money supply was to have two effects.

- First, its eventual implementation would reduce annual inflation rates according to the monetarist theory.
- Second, since everyone was to know what money supply – and hence inflation – would be in the medium term, they would avoid mistakes due to erroneous expectations of inflation.

This second effect depends largely on how convincing the government is. If we all believe that it will actually meet the medium-term financial strategy, then we will form our expectations accordingly; but if we doubt the pre-commitment to the policy or the government's ability to carry it out, then we will form expectations as we always do – mistakenly. The policy of trying to influence expectations in this way can be seen in the context of trying to move the expectations-augmented Phillips curve downwards more quickly (see page 49).

Thus the government tries to be convincing when it announces the medium-term financial strategy.

Monetary policy and monetarist theory

The medium-term financial strategy did not directly control the money supply; rather it set targets for the growth of the money supply and the PSBR. This is not the monetary rule suggested by monetarists such as Professor Friedman (see Chapter 4). In fact control of the money supply had proved almost impossible.

- The banks avoided direct controls by various methods, known collectively as **disintermediation.**
- The Bank of England always met demands for cash from the financial markets by discounting bills; thus attempts to restrict liquidity were ultimately frustrated by the Bank itself.
- Finally, the removal in 1979 of all **exchange controls** on the movements of funds between the UK and other financial markets

meant it was just as easy to borrow 'in Dusseldorf as in Durham' and so controlling credit in the UK would be futile.

The money supply was, therefore, to be controlled by using interest rates, affecting the demand for money, and, as we shall see below, by controlling the size and funding of the PSBR (now called the public sector net cash requirement, or **PSNCR**).

In Chapter 6 we reviewed how raising the rate of interest reduces the demand for money. Figure 26 shows how the official rate of interest has been manipulated frequently to achieve the desired monetary conditions and how other interest rates have moved in line with the official rate.

The role of the PSBR seems more confusing; after all, the budget deficit is a tool of fiscal policy and so apparently outside the scope of a volume on monetary policy. However, there is a relationship between the PSBR and the growth of the money supply *which means that it is essential that fiscal policy supports monetary policy*.

Any lending to the government by banks will inflate the money supply, because the banks will simply create the money they lend.

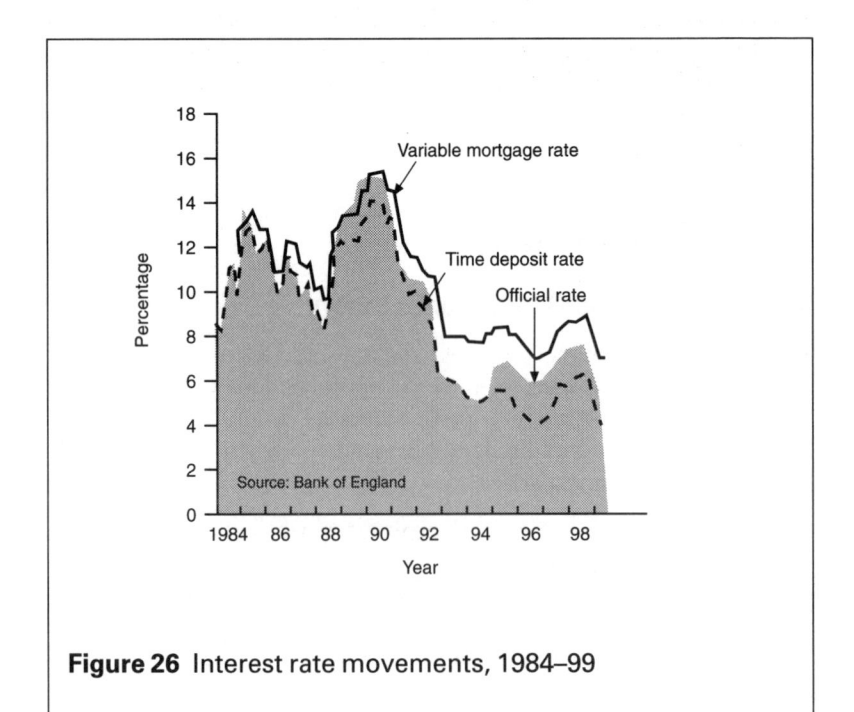

Figure 26 Interest rate movements, 1984–99

However, if any part of the PSBR is financed by the private sector, by selling them bonds, then this does *not* add to the money supply. The PSBR and how it was financed legitimately became part of the medium-term financial strategy, and *fiscal policy had to be designed to meet the needs of monetary policy.*

Funding

One method used to support the medium-term financial strategy was **funding**, which technically refers to the replacement of short-term debt with long-term debt. In Chapter 6 we discussed how it was necessary to influence the market rate of interest in order to support announced changes in the base rate (see page 69). By funding, the Bank of England raised the quantity of long-term debt, forcing the price of such bonds down and so the long-term rate of interest up. This allowed the government to operate its high-interest-rate policy to affect the demand for money. In the mid-1980s the Bank of England **over-funded** the PSBR – i.e. sold more long-term securities than was necessary – creating further upward pressure on interest rates.

From the mid-1980s until the 1993 budget, the government fully funded the PSBR. It issued new long-term debt to the full value of the PSBR (or bought back the equivalent amount of bonds when there was a public sector debt repayment). In this way there could be no money creation, or 'printing of money', to finance the government's budget deficit. The **full-funding rule** was abandoned in 1993 owing to the large size of the PSBR.

Using exchange rates

Around 1985 there was a subtle, but important, shift in policy. The government – whilst still publishing monetary targets – had realized that it was largely not keeping the money supply within the desired target ranges. There was also the disturbing breakdown in the relationship between the money supply and inflation discussed in Chapter 5 (see page 52). Instead the government began using monetary policy to control the exchange rate.

A movement in the exchange rate has important effects on the competitiveness of exports, and so has a direct effect on the real economy. The exchange rate is determined almost exclusively by the *capital account of the balance of payments.* With floating rates and no capital controls, the exchange rate moves to equalize rates of return on domestic and foreign assets, and quite considerable changes in the exchange rate and competitiveness are possible.

The government had realized that the exchange rate reacted to changes in the money supply. A rise in the money supply caused a fall in the rate of interest and this would cause an outflow of capital abroad. The exchange rate would depreciate to correct this, exports becoming more competitive, and so domestic production rising. The higher level of real output causes a rise in the price level and a rise in the demand for money, which in turn causes a rise in the rate of interest. The overall effect of a rise in the money supply had been a *fall* in the exchange rate and a *rise* in the price level.

The aim of the new policy was to tie the pound sterling to the deutschemark (DM). If the exchange rate could be maintained at a constant level, this would imply that the two countries had similar monetary conditions (as there were no forces causing relative changes in their currencies' values). West Germany (as it was then) had a formidably good record on inflation, and so if the £/DM exchange rate could be maintained at a certain level the UK would be enforcing the same monetary conditions as the Germans – and gaining the same benefits of low inflation.

The tool of this monetary policy had to be interest rates, and whenever the exchange rate moved the Bank of England would have to manipulate interest rates to restore the desired exchange rate. Thus if the exchange rate depreciated, this would imply that monetary growth in the UK was higher than in Germany; to reduce monetary growth the rate of interest is raised, money demand falls and the exchange rate is restored.

The exchange rate mechanism (ERM)

The UK entered the exchange rate mechanism of the European Monetary System (EMS) in October 1990. Essentially this was a fixed exchange-rate regime in which the exchange rate of the pound for other European currencies was to be held within a plus or minus 6 per cent band around a central parity of £1/2.95DM. Joining the ERM committed the UK to conducting monetary policy in such a way that would maintain the exchange rate, which meant maintaining interest rates at the level indicated by movements in the exchange rate. The significance of this is two-fold.

- First, in a fixed exchange-rate system the UK inflation rate must not exceed that of other European currencies. If it is higher it will reduce international competitiveness so that excessive wage or price increases will lead to loss of orders, unemployment and idle factories. In other words, *it is an externally imposed discipline on wage and price fixers.*

- Second, by committing itself to a fixed exchange rate the government increases the credibility of its anti-inflation stance. It simply cannot maintain a fixed exchange rate if it issues (or allows to be issued) too much money. *This is tantamount to saying that the government can have either a monetary policy or an exchange rate policy but not both.*

It is partly for this reason that the more committed monetarists, like Margaret Thatcher and Sir Alan Walters, her chief economic advisor who described the ERM as 'half-baked', were so reluctant to enter the ERM. It meant giving up 'discretionary action to control UK money supply' – i.e. giving up monetary policy. To convince the markets that no devaluation would occur, both the government and the Governor of the Bank of England were emphatic in rejecting any such move.

After the ERM

On the 16 September 1992, the pound left the ERM after massive speculative attacks meant that the combined efforts of the European central banks were unable to maintain the agreed parity.

After sterling's departure from the ERM the government needed a new monetary policy. This led to the first example of **inflation targeting** which is the basis of monetary policy today. The Chancellor of the Exchequer, Norman Lamont, announced that the target was now to be to maintain underlying inflation – as measured by RPIX (see page 18) – within a range of 1–4 per cent, with the added proviso that inflation should be in the lower half of the target range by the end of Parliament in 1997. The announcement of the target was accompanied by a number of institutional changes.

A more transparent method of implementing monetary policy was to be established, with monthly meetings between the Chancellor of the Exchequer and the Governor of the Bank of England with senior Treasury and Bank officials. The meetings of this monthly committee would consider all the available evidence, specifically:

- the money supply
- the exchange rate
- producer prices
- house prices
- earnings
- world commodity prices and other factors.

Everything would be taken into account in assessing the outlook for inflation. The minutes of these meetings were to be published to allow all to see how decisions had been arrived at.

Two other changes added to the Bank of England's influence:

- It was announced that the Bank in future would publish a quarterly **Inflation Report**. The role of this report was to enable the Bank to publish its own inflation forecasts and to state publicly when it believed that inflation was likely to head outside the government's target range.
- The Bank was given control over the precise *timing* of interest rate changes, although only after a decision to change the rates had been taken by the Chancellor.

Inflation remained the primary target, but the basis on which decisions were made was not linked to one specific factor. The Bank of England promoted debate on the use of inflation targets, what measure of inflation should be used, and which inflationary 'shocks' could be ignored and which not.

In May 1997 the new Labour government decided that it was time to change the way in which monetary policy was implemented. The current arrangements are the subject of Chapter 8.

KEY WORDS

Bretton Woods system
Prices and incomes policies
Credit controls
Social Contract
Medium-term financial strategy
PSBR/PSNCR

Disintermediation
Exchange controls
Funding
Over-funded
Full-funding rule
Inflation targeting

Further reading

Buxton, T., Chapman, P. and Temple, P., Chapter 3 in *Britain's Economic Performance*, 2nd edn, Routledge, 1998.

Griffiths, A. and Wall, S.(eds), Chapter 18 in *Applied Economics*, 7th edn, Addison-Wesley Longman, 1997.

Hare, P. and Simpson, L., Chapter 12 in *UK Economy: Performance and Policy*, 2nd edn, Prentice Hall/Harvester Wheatsheaf, 1996.

Sloman, J., Chapter 20 in *Economics*, Prentice Hall, 1997.

Useful website

HM Treasury: www.hm-treasury.gov.uk/

Essay questions
1. (a) Explain the differences between monetary policy and fiscal policy. [10 marks]
   (b) Discuss the changes in the aims and methods of monetary policy in recent years. [15 marks]
2. Assess the economic implication of the use of monetary policy to keep inflation below a target rate. [40 marks] [University of Oxford Delegacy of Local Examinations 1999]

Data response question
This task is based on a question set by the University of Oxford Delegacy of Local Examinations in 1998. Study Table A and then answer the questions that follow, using your knowledge of economics and economic analysis.

Table A Money growth and inflation in the UK

Year	Annual growth of M4 monetary aggregate (%)	Retail prices annual change (inflation) (%)
1988	17.7	4.9
1989	18.4	7.8
1990	15.8	9.5
1991	7.6	5.9
1992	4.0	3.7
1993	3.0	1.6
1994	5.1	2.5
1995	7.5	3.4

Source: *National Institute Economic Review*, October 1996.

1. From your studies, and using the data in Table A, discuss the relationship between changes in the M4 measure of the money supply and inflation. [14 marks]
2. Is the government currently following a restrictionist or an expansionary monetary policy? Explain your answer. [6 marks]

Chapter Eight
Current UK monetary policy

'*My intention is to lock into our policymaking system a commitment to consistently low inflation in the long term.*'
Gordon Brown, Chancellor of the Exchequer, 1998

On the election of the Labour government in May 1997, monetary policy was put on a new footing. The arrangements were formalized by the Bank of England Act in 1998 and this chapter examines those current monetary policy arrangements.

Institutional arrangements

The radical change to policy was to give the Bank of England independence to set interest rates. The new arrangement took decisions on the level of interest rates out of the hands of the politicians and Treasury. The Bank was given an inflation target to meet and a **Monetary Policy Committee** (MPC) was established at the Bank to take interest rate decisions. *It is the job of the MPC to maintain price stability by the use of monetary policy.*

The MPC is made up of Bank of England representatives and Treasury appointments (see the boxed item).

Each member of the committee has a vote, with the Governor having a casting vote in the event of a tie. A Treasury representative attends the meetings of the MPC to convey the views of the Treasury when appropriate, but that person does not have any voting rights.

Policy objectives

The Bank of England Act states that the objectives of monetary policy shall be:

- to maintain price stability
- subject to that, to support the economic policy of the government, including its objectives for growth and employment.

Price stability is as defined by the Chancellor of the Exchequer. So far this has been done by the use of an inflation target of 2.5 per cent on the RPIX measure – that is the RPI excluding mortgage interest payments – although some variability is allowed. It is envisaged that, although the target can be changed each year at the time of the budget, it will remain at 2.5 per cent for the 'foreseeable future'.

> **MEMBERS OF THE
> MONETARY POLICY COMMITTEE**
>
> The nine members of the MPC are currently as follows.
>
> The Governor of the Bank of England – Eddie George
> Deputy Governor responsible for monetary policy – Mervyn King
> Deputy Governor responsible for financial stability – David Clementi
> Officer responsible for monetary policy analysis – John Vickers
> Officer responsible for monetary operations – Ian Plenderleith
> Four members appointed by the Chancellor of the Exchequer
>
> *The Chancellor's nominees must have 'knowledge or experience which is likely to be relevant to the committee's functions'. These were initially:*
>
> Sir Alan Budd – formerly Chief Economic Adviser at the Treasury
> Willem Buiter – Cambridge University
> Charles Goodhart – London School of Economics
> DeAnne Julius – formerly Chief Economist at British Airways

It is recognized that there may be shocks to the economy that will cause inflation to vary from its target, so the MPC is given a range of one percentage point on either side of the target. If RPIX inflation is more than 3.5 per cent or less than 1.5 per cent, then the Governor of the Bank of England, as chairman of the MPC, must write an open letter to the Chancellor explaining why this has occurred and what action is to be taken to rectify the situation.

Notice that inflation being too low is just as unacceptable as it being too high. Thus the MPC have no incentive to maintain interest rates at a high level.

The aim of the policy is *price stability* – which is not defined as an inflation rate of zero. Some inflation is seen as being acceptable as this allows for changes in relative prices, the introduction of new goods, improved quality and exchange rate movements. However, price stability is seen as *a precondition for high and stable levels of growth and employment.* The policy is not simply one of low inflation for its own sake, but for the overall economic benefits it can bring.

Given the concerns about output and employment if inflation does deviate from target, then the MPC may take measures that take longer than is strictly necessary to return it to 2.5 per cent. This would be to avoid the large fluctuations in output and employment that more radical action might cause. As such, the MPC is not called upon to be *'inflation nutters'* but to take a wider and longer term view.

The policymaking process

The policymaking process is not based on any one theory of inflation, nor one policy idea. In this sense it is unusual and complicated. The MPC looks at a range of possible sources of inflation and balances the risks from each to reach a conclusion on the likely future path of the RPIX. The committee then adjusts its only policy tool, the rate of interest, if that is deemed to be necessary.

Figure 27 shows a highly simplified flow chart of the MPC's actions. Every three months the MPC publishes the *Inflation Report*, which it took over as its report from May 1997. In the *Inflation Report* it sets out the members' views on inflation, the important influences on it at present, and the risks for the future. The report also includes a forecast for inflation and GDP growth in the form of a fan chart (see later).

- **The three-monthly predictive cycle**

Although the MPC meets monthly and publishes a decision on interest rates, it is best to focus on the prediction of inflation contained in the *Inflation Report* as a way of understanding how the MPC operates.

Central to the approach is that policy and other events affect inflation with a lag, as discussed on page 72. Where changes in the money supply and inflation are concerned this lag can be two years (see Chapter 4). For other variables, such as wage inflation and the exchange rate, the lag is shorter. Owing to the existence of these variable and imprecise lags, it is not sensible to react simply to the current level of inflation, but to the *likely future level*. Thus the MPC works with a forecast of inflation two years into the future.

The MPC process recognizes that there are many factors that can affect inflation and that not all of these are important all of the time. For example, sometimes a depreciating exchange rate will exert inflationary pressure on the economy, but at other times the greatest danger will be rising wage costs. Usually there are competing influences on inflation and these must be balanced to form a view on the most likely course inflation will take.

Figure 27 shows that the MPC takes regular account of a number of variables – listed in the 'regular data' box. These are organized in order of the lag with which they feed through to inflation, monetary

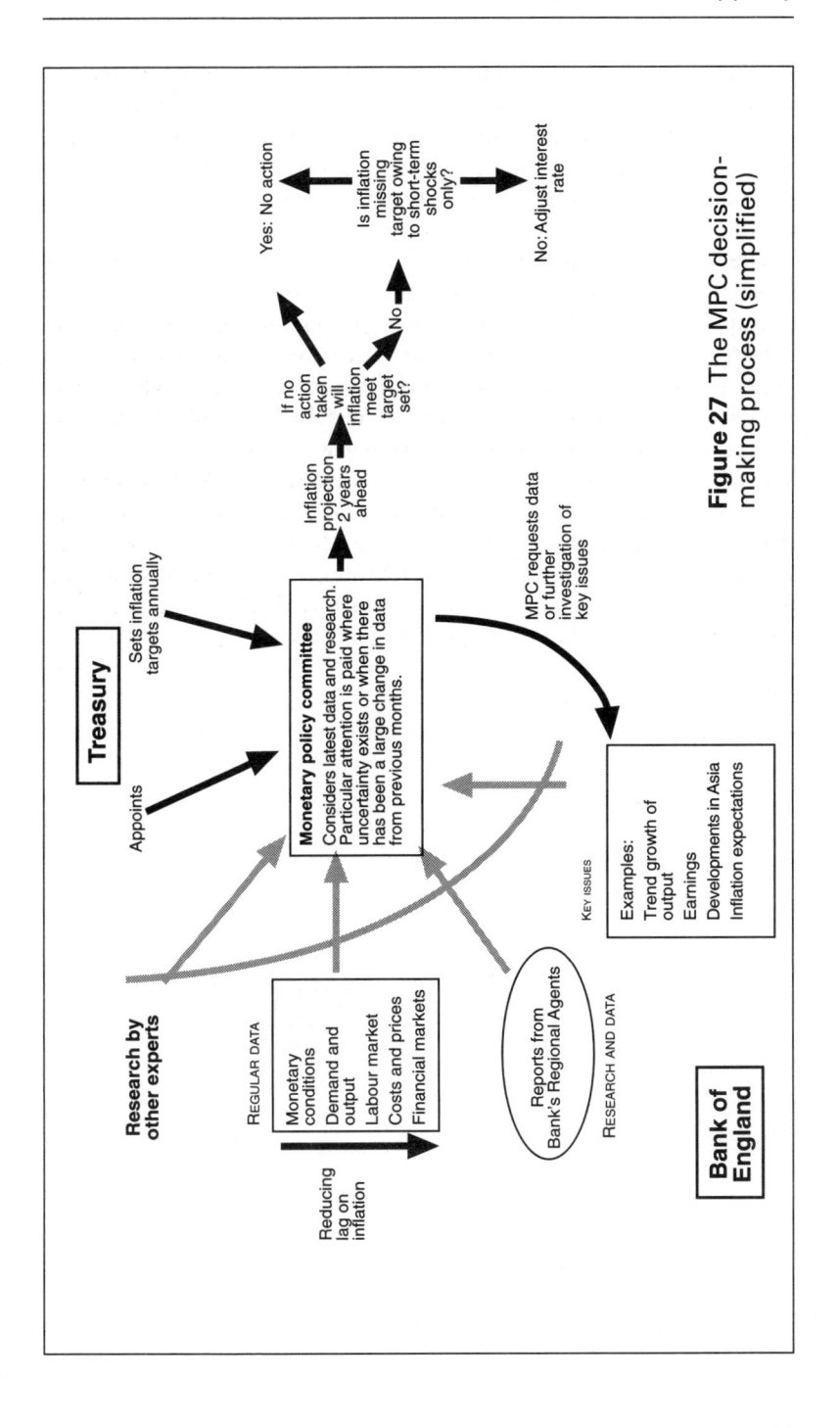

Current UK monetary policy

Figure 27 The MPC decision-making process (simplified)

conditions having the longest lag. There is no presumption of importance in the ordering of this list; and although the MPC has recognized that *'inflation is a monetary phenomenon in the long run'*, the committee cannot be categorized as belonging to a particular school of thought – such as monetarist or Keynesian – on the cause(s) of inflation.

The MPC also asks Bank of England staff to investigate particular 'key issues' that may affect inflation in each prediction cycle. For example, in 1998 the problems (among others) of Asian and Russian debt restructuring were given special attention. In addition the MPC hears the views of the Bank's twelve Regional Agents who are in regular contact with over 7000 firms in the UK. They give the MPC the information they have collected from UK firms from around the country and provide an important point of contact with industry. The MPC also takes account of the views of academics and research organizations independent of the Bank.

Having reviewed all of the data after a series of meetings, the MPC uses a variety of computer models and its own judgement to form a view on the likely path of RPIX inflation over the next two years. A

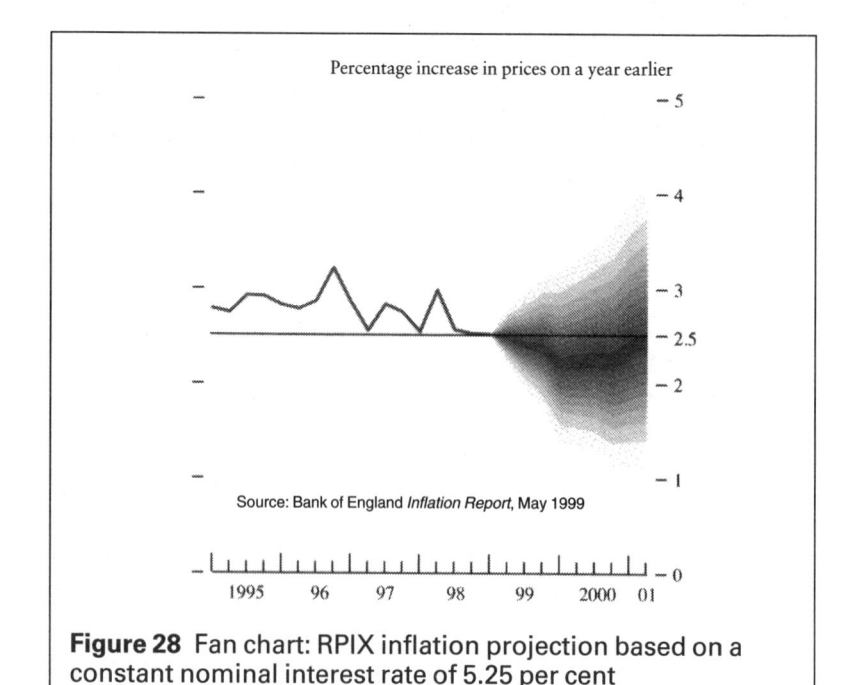

Figure 28 Fan chart: RPIX inflation projection based on a constant nominal interest rate of 5.25 per cent

Current UK monetary policy

forecast of GDP growth is published as well. These projections are produced in the form of **fan charts**, an example of which is shown in Figure 28.

- **Interest rate decisions**

Suppose the initial prediction shows that RPIX inflation will deviate significantly from the target rate if interest rates are left unchanged. The MPC must decide whether this is due to short-term shocks that, if no action is taken, will return RPIX inflation to target. An example of such a shock occurred in 1998 when a second budget occurred within 12 months of the previous one, resulting in two rises in excise duties – such as the tax on petrol – in the index leading to a measured rise in retail prices. This caused RPIX to increase, but fall back again once the first rise in duties fell out of the year-on-year calculation.

If the MPC decides that inflation is missing the target rate as a result of such a short-term shock, then it need take no action. If the deviation is not due to short-term factors, then the committee must consider the effect of changing interest rates. If the MPC judges that the risk to inflation is upwards, then it will raise interest rates, thereby hoping to reduce demand, possibly cause the exchange rate to rise and increase the cost of credit.

The size of the interest rate change will depend on how great the MPC judges the risk of inflation to be, and by how much inflation is likely to overshoot the target rate. A cut in the rate of interest will be announced if the MPC believes RPIX inflation will undershoot the target.

- **Monthly meetings**

The analysis above suggests that decisions are taken only at the time of the preparation of the *Inflation Report*, but in fact decisions are made each month at a two-day meeting of the MPC.

The fan-chart forecasts that are made quarterly are used as the basis for decision-making, but as circumstances change then the MPC can change its view on the risks of inflation. If its members deem that circumstances have changed sufficiently, then they will adjust the interest rate.

The interest rate decision is announced at noon on the second day of the monthly meeting and the minutes of the meeting are published shortly afterwards.

- **How interest rates are influenced for the whole economy**

The interest rate over which the MPC has control is the Bank of

England's **repo rate** – the rate at which the Bank will lend money to the banking system with gilt-edged securities (government bonds) used as security.

The Bank of England influences short-term interest rates by varying the cost to the banking system of obtaining cash. Banks require cash to fulfil their daily transactions but do not always have sufficient cash to meet their needs. To obtain cash funds from the Bank of England, banks have two options.

Firstly, they can sell bills before they are due for repayment. These bills are bought at a discount on their redemption value, and exactly how much of a discount depends on the rate of interest applied.

Alternatively the commercial banks can enter into a 'gilt repo' agreement. This is essentially a loan whereby the commercial bank agrees to sell the Bank of England gilts and to repurchase an equivalent amount at a future date at an agreed price. The repo rate is then the rate of interest applied to this loan which is secured against the gilts used as security. The rate at which bills are discounted is directly linked to the repo rate.

As the financial institutions must pay this repo rate to obtain funds, if it rises the higher cost is passed on to their customers. It can be viewed, therefore, as the lowest rate in a structure of interest rates. If it falls, they all fall; if it rises, they all rise – rather like a raft rising and falling with the tide.

Understanding the fan chart

The fan chart is a way of displaying the MPC's views on the risk of inflation. It shows the calculated *probability* of inflation lying in a particular range. The use of such charts demonstartes two points:

- there is uncertainty about the course of future inflation
- the risks of inflation need not be symmetrical – the risk of inflation being above the central prediction may be more or less than the risk of it being below the prediction.

The fan chart can be thought of as a contour map. The darkest region is the central projection (or highest probability path) of inflation. It covers just one-tenth of the total probability. The increasingly lighter regions that surround it show paths that are considered decreasingly likely. The two bands on each side of the darkest band contain the next one-tenth most likely rates, and so on up to 90 per cent.

Note that the chart gets wider – fans out – reflecting the truism that the further into the future the prediction, the less sure we can be about where inflation will be. In Figure 28, which shows a May 1999 fan chart, the MPC is saying that it believes that there is a one-tenth (i.e. one-in-ten) chance that inflation will be about 2.5 per cent in March 2001, and there is a nine-tenths chance that it will be between 4.1 and 1.2 per cent. These are the limits of the 'shaded' area (the outer bands are very feint in the figure reproduced here).

It is clear from the shape of the inflation chart in Figure 28 that, at that time, the MPC judged the risks of inflation being below the target rate at the end of 1999 to be higher than the risk of going above the target. By March 2001, the prediction was that the rate was practically equally likely to be above as below the target of 2.5 per cent. *The important point is that the fan chart reflects the balance of risks as perceived by the MPC and it is this balance that determines policy decisions.*

The rationale for current policy

There are four basic reasons for introducing the new policy:

- The real world works best when inflation is under control.
- Inflation can be generated by a variety of sources which, in an open economy like the UK, vary in importance over time.
- Governments have objectives other than price stability and may be tempted to trade off higher inflation to achieve them.
- Political control over economic policy cannot be completely surrendered to an unelected body.

We shall examine each reason in turn.

- **Benefits of price stability**

Inflation causes disruption in the price system. As we saw in Chapter 3, there can be significant costs associated with inflation. An inefficient market can lead to lower output and growth, and so can the effects of monetary policy aimed at controlling inflation. If inflation is highly variable then it is also likely that monetary policy will raise and lower interest rates significantly leading to greater output variability.

- **Inflation can have many sources**

The view that dominated the period to the 1980s was that inflation had a particular cause. In the 1960s it was high aggregate demand or cost-push factors, in the 1970s and early 80s it was the rising money supply. The new arrangements reflect the view that inflation can originate from many different sources.

The MPC looks at two broad categories: domestically generated inflation and externally generated inflation. In the former, movements in the money supply, wage inflation, the labour market and domestic credit are all examples of potential causes of rises in the price level.

Import prices and the exchange rate are examples of external factors that can influence the price level. Approximately 20 per cent of the RPIX is attributable to import prices.

The members of the MPC are provided with data on over 1000 variables.

- **Governments may be tempted to allow inflation to rise**

As we have seen there is, at least in the short term, a trade-off between inflation and unemployment. Governments are expected to deliver a high level of output and employment and are rewarded when they do by re-election. Thus a government may be tempted to promote higher levels of output and employment when an election approaches. Because monetary policy affects inflation only with a lag, this leads to higher inflation only later, after the election, and so requires higher interest rates to reduce it again.

This is sometimes called the **political business cycle** and leads to unacceptable variability in inflation and GDP. Thus taking decisions on monetary policy out of the hands of politicians prevents such temptations.

By giving the central bank an inflation target and price stability as its primary goal, more consistent policy should arise leading to less fluctuation in inflation and output.

- **Some public accountability must be retained**

The Bank of England has not been given total independence. The Bank has what is known as **instrument independence**. It is free to manipulate the instruments of policy, but it does not have **goal independence** which is still set by the Treasury.

The Bank of England cannot therefore decide what price stability means by itself, nor can it ignore the government's other economic policy aims which it must support. If the government decides that it wishes to see less or more inflation it simply changes the inflation target. If it believes the MPC is not carrying out its duties properly it appoints new members. The government gets elected or not on its overall record.

The MPC is also held accountable in other ways. The *Inflation Report* and monthly minutes of the MPC are regular and transparent records of what it does and why it took the decisions it did. The Court of the Bank of England (like the board of directors for most banks) receives a regular monthly report and must supervise the MPC with particular regard to the proper collection of regional and sectoral information. Further, the MPC can be required to give evidence to the Treasury Select Committee of the House of Commons.

The vote of each member of the MPC is recorded and published in the minutes. Thus each member of the MPC is individually responsible for keeping to the inflation target.

Criticisms of the MPC approach

- **An inflation target is not enough**

Some commentators have claimed that an inflation target is too narrow and that consideration should be given to other variables. The variables suggested are wide, such as money supply, GDP and real GDP.

Targeting other single variables, such as the money supply, has already been tried and found wanting. Concern over the level of output is a legitimate concern of all 'right minded people' as the Governor of the Bank of England stated.

The Bank also publishes a projection for GDP growth with its inflation forecast (see Figure 29). This is because the Bank recognizes that not only are GDP and inflation related, but that it is a fundamental aim of policy to keep the demand side of the economy in balance with

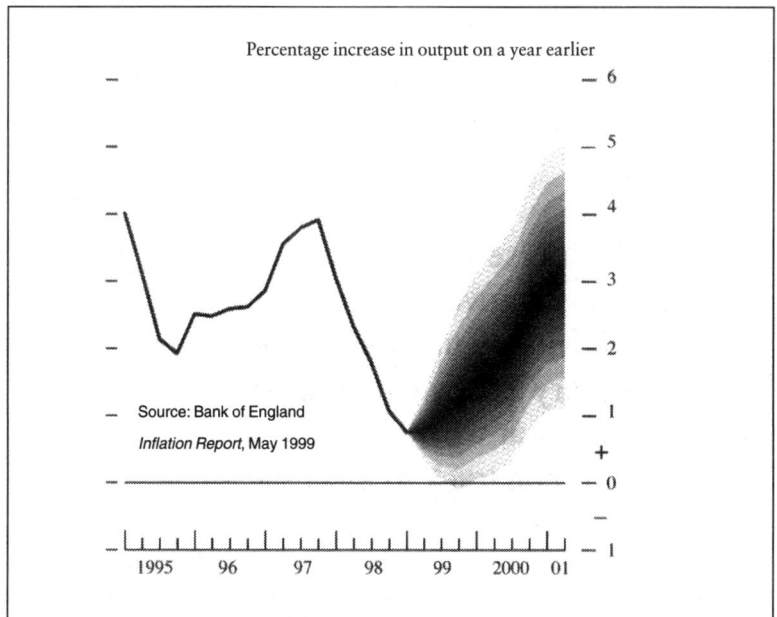

Figure 29 Fan chart: GDP projection based on a constant nominal interest rate of 5.25 per cent

the supply side. Monetary policy is a demand-side tool and the long-term aim of price stability and high and sustainable growth depends on ensuring that the demand side of the economy does not exceed the supply side's ability to meet that demand. Thus, argues the Bank, concern for the level and volatility of output growth is a fundamental part of its approach.

- Fine control of inflation is not possible

Many critics argue that the time lags involved in the operation of monetary policy, and the economy's highly complex nature, make the interest rate too clumsy a tool to regulate the economy. They point out that policymakers do not have superior information about the future cyclical movements of the economy, nor do they know where the 'natural rate' of output is. Therefore their attempts to regulate the economy will usually make things worse owing to inappropriate actions and timings of action.

The policymakers accept that their forecasts are not perfect; indeed the fan chart explicitly recognizes this by showing many *probability* bands. They argue, however, that they are using a medium-term approach taking account of all available information. Further, they are not trying to keep inflation at the target rate at all times.

- The MPC is not truly independent

One of the advantages sought by the new arrangements is to give monetary policy and the commitment to price stability greater credibility by having an independent (i.e. non-political) body responsible for setting interest rates. Many argue that the MPC is not really independent of the government.

The Governor of the Bank of England is appointed by the Chancellor of the Exchequer, as are the four 'other members' of the MPC. A majority of the MPC are, therefore, easily replaced if they do not satisfy government aims.

The Chancellor can set the inflation target that defines price stability every year at whatever level the government wishes. Thus a government seeking re-election might be prepared to raise the target and the MPC will be obliged to try to meet it.

A Treasury representative attends the MPC meetings. This representative can give the government's view. For example, the government may have a view that it wishes the MPC to take a longer period to restore price stability in order to avoid output and employment variability. This can be viewed as a good or bad thing.

Certainly the press has portrayed the MPC as poodles of the

Chancellor when they reduced interest rates in late 1998 following widespread calls for cuts from industry and trade unions. The Matt cartoon appeared the day after the decision was announced.

In their defence the MPC argue that the process is transparent and in the public domain. The MPC members form their opinions about the most likely path of inflation in their view and implement the policy they think will achieve the inflation target they are given. Their view on the future path of inflation and their reasons for thinking this are published and cannot be influenced by appeals from any quarter. If they adjusted interest rates to a level that was inconsistent with their view of inflation, or doctored their prediction in the fan chart, everybody would see this immediately.

- **The MPC members as a group are 'inflation nutters'**

This rather unkind comment has been put forward to say that the MPC cares only about the achievement of the inflation target and is prepared to abandon workers and firms to their fate.

As has already been shown, inflation is not viewed in isolation. Output and growth are part of the committee's remit, although these are its secondary consideration. The MPC is charged to achieve the inflation target it is given, not one its members chose themselves.

- **The MPC members need real world experience**

The MPC is made up of Bank officials and mainly academic economists. Trade union and industry leaders have called for more members of the committee to have industrial experience so that they can react to the needs of the trading and manufacturing sectors. They argue that the MPC's primary concern with inflation makes it ignore the needs of these groups.

It is difficult to give much credibility to these views, although at any one time it is likely that some sectors of the economy, be they regions or particular industries, will be faring less well than others. A number of points can be made.

The call for 'real world experience' is only a call for members of one **vested interest group** to be represented on the committee. In fact the committee is there to make decisions free of vested interest. Each member of the MPC must pursue the inflation target they have been given, not one of their own. But that is what the calls essentially are asking for. They are asking the committee to trade off some inflation for short-term gains in employment in particular sectors. As we have seen, this could easily lead to longer term losses in employment if inflation accelerates away. Also, a major reason for the establishment of the MPC was to take decisions out of the hands of people – the government – who might be tempted to serve their own interests by the manipulation of policy.

Summing up

Inflation targeting began in the UK in October 1992, but has only been pursued in its present form since 1997. It is too soon to form conclusions about the success of the policy. So far inflation has been remarkably stable by recent standards, but this may be just luck.

The new policy arrangements mean that a far more sophisticated view on the causes of inflation is adopted. It is no longer possible to characterize policy by the labels used in Chapters 4 and 7. It will be necessary to watch how the MPC reacts to the economic situation and the reasons it gives for its actions.

So far the committee has proved to be quite active, raising interest rates as the balance of risks appeared to be upwards and quickly down again when the risks appeared to reverse. The period June to November in 1998 is a good example of such activism. Monetary policy is a medium-term strategy, however, and it is important to focus on the process and rationale of policy to understand it, not the immediate reactions of the popular press on a week-by-week basis.

KEY WORDS

Monetary policy committee
Fan charts
Political business cycle
Repo rate

Instrument independence
Goal independence
Vested interest group

Further reading
Atkinson, B., Livesey, F. and Milward, R., Chapter 21 in *Applied Economics*, Macmillan, 1998.

Ball, J., Chapter 4 in *The British Economy at the Crossroads*, FT/Pitman, 1998.

Grant, S., Chapter 34 in *Stanlake's Introductory Economics*, Longman, 1999.

Smith, D., Chapter 4 in *UK Current Economic Policy*, Heinemann Educational, 1999.

Useful website
Bized – virtual economy allows visitors to design and test their own economic policy. It includes different inflation targets for the MPC: www.bized.ac.uk

Essay questions
1. (a) Explain the various costs of inflation. [12 marks]
   (b) Discuss the proposition that, if the economy is to prosper in the long run, the main objective of government policy should be to control inflation. [13 marks] [Associated Examining Board 1998]
2. Evaluate the policies that government may take to reduce inflation, in the short run and long run. [40 marks] [University of Oxford Delegacy of Local Examinations 1998]

Data response question
This task is based on a question set by the Oxford & Cambridge board in 1996. Study Figures A to D (taken from Bank of England *Inflation Reports*) and then answer the questions that follow, using your knowledge of economics and economic analysis.

Figure A Measures of annual inflation

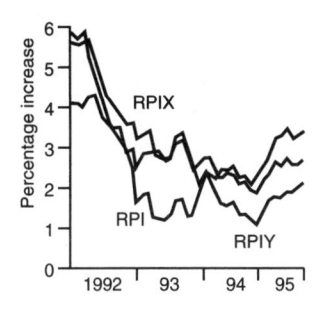

Figure B Annual earnings growth

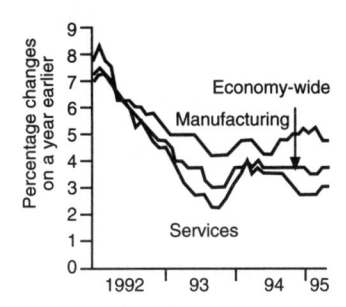

Inflation and UK Monetary Policy

Figure C Manufacturers' prices

Figure D Consumers' expenditure and retail sales

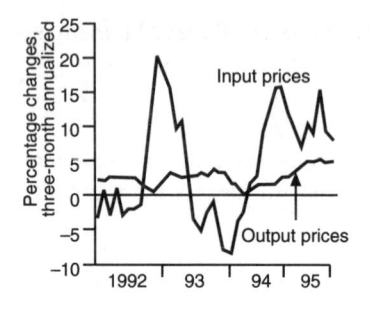

(a) Latest three months on the same three months in the previous year.

(b) Latest quarter on the same quarter in the previous year.

1. What is the difference between RPI, RPIX and RPIY as measures of inflation (Figure A)? [3 marks]
2. Why, since 1994, has inflation measured by the RPI been greater than inflation measured by either the RPIX or the RPIY? [2 marks]
3. Why are annual increases in manufacturing earnings invariably greater than those in services (Figure B)? [2 marks]
4. Explain why manufacturers' input prices fluctuate more than output prices (Figure C). [3 marks]
5. On the basis of the evidence provided in the four graphs, was the Bank of England right to argue, in the summer of 1995, for an increase in interest rates? [9 marks]
6. What further information would help to determine the strength or weakness of the Bank's case? [6 marks]

Chapter Nine
The wider impact of monetary policy

'*British interest rates have been cut from 7.5 per cent in October to 5.25 per cent now. This has done much to convince Britons that the sky is not about to fall in.*'
The Economist, 24 April 1999

Both inflation and monetary policy impact on the whole of the economy and on particular sections of it. In Chapter 3 we looked at some of the costs and benefits of inflation from the point of view of the economy. In this chapter we shall be examining the impact of monetary policy on households and firms.

Aggregate demand

As we have seen, the conduct of monetary policy means changing interest rates. If interest rates are raised, the aggregate demand curve shifts to the left; if interest rates fall, the aggregate demand curve shifts to the right.

Recall that aggregate demand is made up of various components, including consumers' expenditure (approximately two-thirds of GDP) and investment. Both of these are affected by changes in the rate of interest. If the rate of interest rises then it is more expensive to borrow. Fewer loans will be taken out by consumers and firms, thus reducing aggregate demand. Borrowers will also find that they will have to repay more on existing loans, further reducing the available income to spend on current goods and services. This can be shown in the AD/AS model.

Following a rise in the rate of interest we can expect the level of consumption and investment to fall. This causes the aggregate demand curve to shift to the left, from AD_1 to AD_2 in Figure 30, leading to a lower level of real output, Y_2, and a lower price level, P_2. Whilst clearly this is anti-inflationary there is a cost in terms of lost output and employment.

Monetary policy and households

The main source of household income is payment from employment (some households receive transfer payments and receive income from investments). Households then decide how to spend this income, and monetary policy has a major impact upon these decisions.

Inflation and UK Monetary Policy

Figure 30 The effect of a rise in interest rates

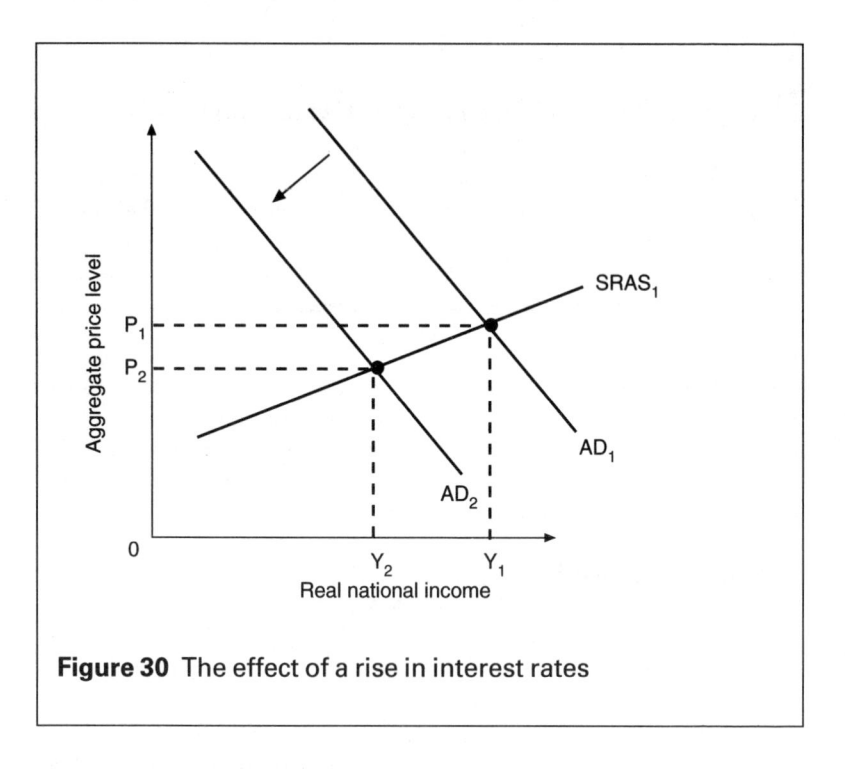

Let us suppose that a typical household has a current income and owns some assets, such as a house on which they have an outstanding mortgage. They receive their income every month, but their assets have a particular value which can rise or fall. How well-off the household is depends upon a combination of their flow of income each month and their stock of wealth. The better off the household feels, the more they will spend on current consumption.

- Savings decisions

Interest rates are a major influence on the decisions of households about how much of their current income to spend. If a household decides to save some of its current income it must consider it worth giving up consumption now for the chance of consuming more later.

The return paid on **savings** is therefore an important factor, because if interest rates rise then households may feel that it is now worth putting off some more consumption now in order to consume even more later. When interest rates are raised, therefore, we can expect some consumption to be delayed and aggregate demand to fall.

● Mortgage payments

For a household buying a home with borrowed money, the **mortgage repayments** can form a considerable proportion of monthly expenditure, especially in the early years of repayment.

In 1998, more than three-quarters of mortgages in the UK were of the variable-rate type, whereby if interest rates are changed then mortgage rates also change. As Figure 31 shows, mortgage rates fluctuated considerably over the period 1989–98, ranging from 15.5 to 7 per cent. Table 4 shows the implications of this fluctuation.

Figure 31 Mortgage rates, 1989–98

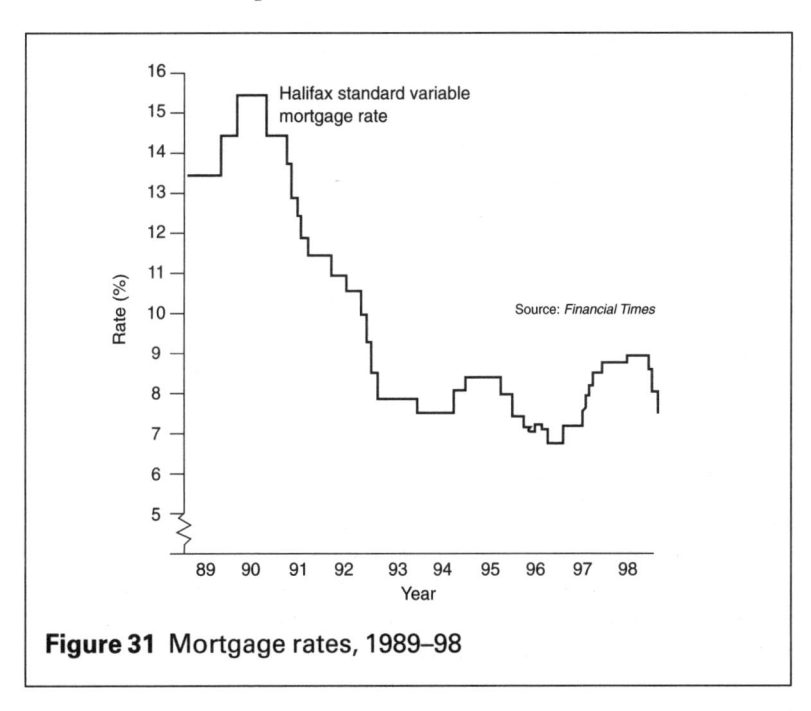

Table 4 The effect of interest rates on mortgage repayments

| | Monthly repayments at each mortgage rate | | | |
Loan size	7%	10%	12.5%	15.5%
£30 000	£157.50	£225.00	£281.25	£348.75
£60 000	£332.50	£475.00	£593.75	£736.25
£100 000	£565.84	£808.34.00	£1010.42	£1252.93

Based on a Halifax building society endowment mortgage, December 1998.

Inflation and UK Monetary Policy

The average new mortgage for borrowers in the UK in 1998 was approximately £60 000, while average household income was approximately £18 000. At 7 per cent the mortgage repayments would represent 22 per cent of pre-tax income, rising to 49 per cent when the rate is 15.5 per cent. For an average household from November 1990 to December 1993, their mortgage payments would have declined £375.25 a month at 1998 prices.

From this it can be seen that a change in interest rates can have a profound effect on a household's **discretionary income** – income left over after mortgage payments. This will feed through into the rest of the economy, reducing demand and so output and employment.

- ### The housing market

The effect of changing interest rates is felt especially strongly in the market for housing. As a modest rise in interest rates can lead to a substantial increase in monthly mortgage repayments, the decision of households to move, or buy, a new house will be heavily influenced by changes in monetary policy.

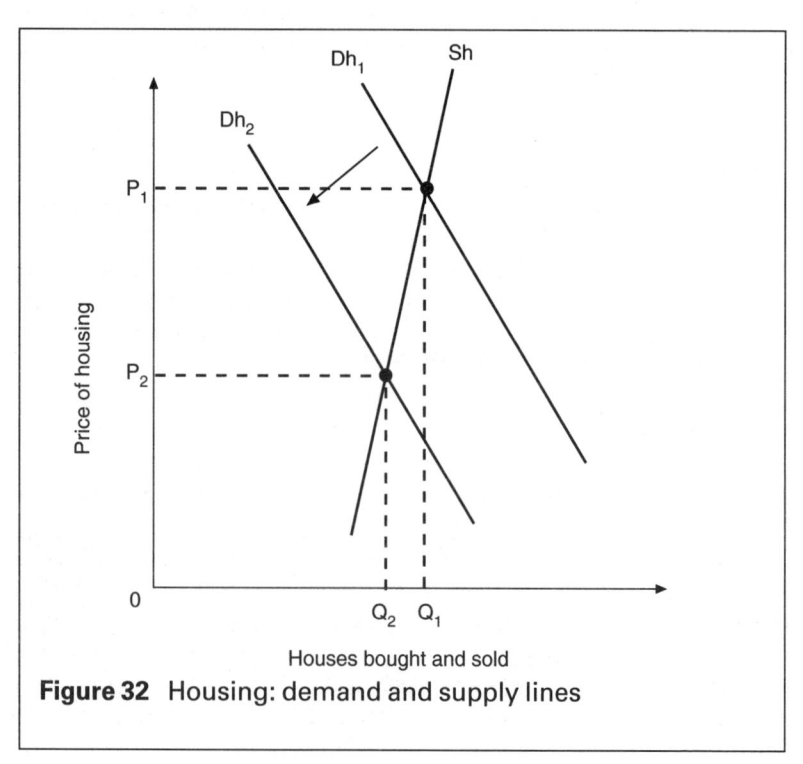

Figure 32 Housing: demand and supply lines

The combined effect of higher repayments and a generally lower level of discretionary income caused by the rise in interest rates causes the demand curve for housing to shift to the left. In Figure 32 the supply of housing (Sh) is shown to be relatively price-inelastic. A shift in the demand curve for houses, from Dh_1 to Dh_2, therefore causes the price of houses to change significantly.

- Asset prices

For most households their main asset is their home. As we have now seen, interest rates will affect the value (price) of this asset significantly, falling when interest rates rise and rising when they fall. In Chapter 6 we saw that the value of interest-bearing assets also falls as interest rates rise.

This implies that the value of **household assets** will generally fall as interest rates rise, and this will make the household feel less well-off as the value of their wealth has declined. This will often mean that they decide to spend less on current goods and services.

For households with no mortgage and significant savings, a rise in interest rates will make them better off as they receive higher incomes from their assets. In general, however, the net effect in the UK is for there to be a fall in household demand when interest rates rise, as net borrowers tend to have a higher marginal propensity to consume than net savers.

Monetary policy and firms

Firms will be affected both directly and indirectly by the operation of monetary policy. Household decisions affect demand for firms' products and this will feed through to all enterprises in the economy. Interest rates have a direct effect on firms' costs, the prospects for the economy, firms' investment decisions, and the exchange rate.

- Costs

Virtually all firms have outstanding loans. The most common type of loan is an overdraft, which is a negative balance on the firm's bank account; and many have long term loans. In the UK a large percentage of these loans have variable rates of interest.

As we have seen, when interest rates rise they have a substantial effect on mortgage repayments. Firms are affected in exactly the same way. If interest rates rise they must pay higher interest charges – a rise in fixed costs – and this will squeeze their cash flow and reduce their profit margin.

In response to this, firms may be induced to raise their prices, further reducing sales (for most goods and services). Often this is not possible

ILLUSTRATION OF THE EFFECT OF INTEREST RATES ON PROFITABILITY

The investment project costing £100 000 repays over three years the following amounts:

Year 1: £40 000   Year 2: £40 000   Year 3: £40 000

If the real interest rate is 8 per cent, the outcome is:

Year	Loan interest	Real income	Outstanding debt
1	£8000	£40 000	£68 000
2	£5440	£40 000	£33 440
3	£2675	£40 000	+£3 885

At the end of the project a profit of £3885 has been made. If the firm expects real interest rates of 8 per cent it will invest.

If the real interest rate is 10 per cent, the outcome is:

Year	Loan interest	Real income	Outstanding debt
1	£10 000	£40 000	£70 000
2	£7 000	£40 000	£37 000
3	£3 700	£40 000	£700

At the end of the project the firm has an outstanding debt of £700. If the firm expects a real interest rate of 10 per cent it will not undertake the investment.

owing to the amount of competition from domestic and foreign firms. Firms may also cut back on expenditure, such as investment, or may find the burden of debt too great and cease trading. Of course, falls in interest rates have the opposite effect and are welcomed.

- Investment

Investment by firms is highly dependent on two factors:

- the **expected real rate of interest**, and
- the **expected rate of profit**.

The expected real rate of interest

The real rate of interest is defined as the nominal rate of interest minus inflation. If a firm is charged 10 per cent interest on any loan it takes out and the rate of inflation is also 10 per cent, then the real rate of interest is zero. Say the loan is £1000 for one year. During this period the purchasing power of money has declined by 10 per cent, and so in effect the firm has repaid only the amount it originally borrowed in real terms.

The wider impact of monetary policy

Figure 33 The investment demand curve

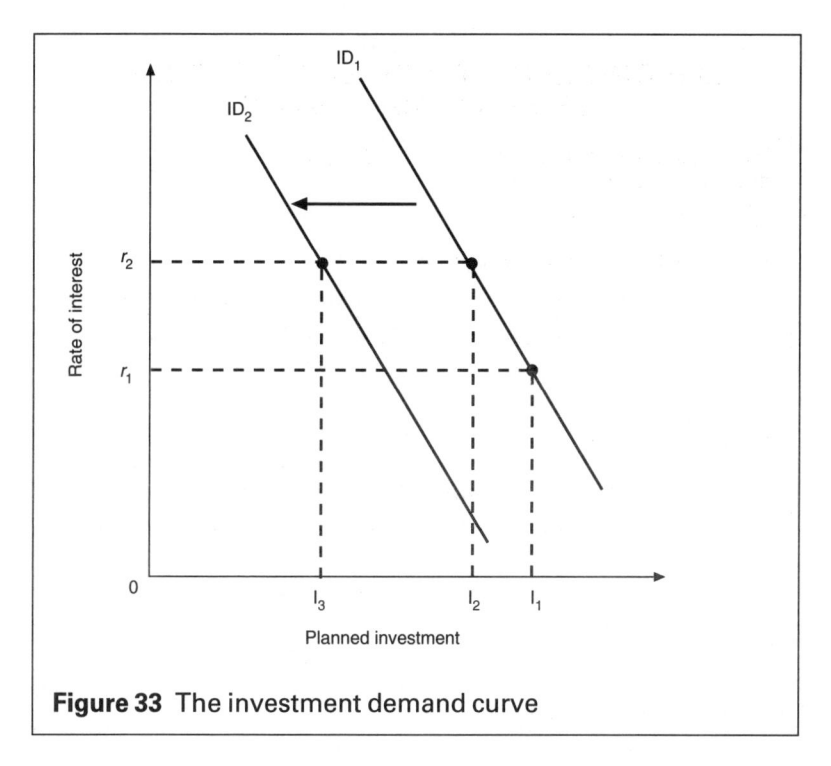

The lower the real rate of interest, the more investment projects are worth undertaking. Consider a project that will require a £100 000 investment and will return in each of the next three years £40 000 in real terms; after this the project ceases and there are no assets left to sell.

If we ignore interest payments, this investment appears to yield a real profit of £20 000. Interest rates are of significance.

The boxed item shows how, at a real rate of interest of 8 per cent, the project makes a profit of £3885. When real interest rates reach 10 per cent the project becomes unprofitable.

Thus when interest rates rise the amount of investment undertaken by firms will fall. This can be shown by the investment demand curve as illustrated in Figure 33. As the rate of interest rises from r_1 to r_2 there is a movement along the investment demand curve ID_1 and the level of investment planned by firms falls from I_1 to I_2. This will cause the level of aggregate demand in the economy to fall, resulting in a lower level of output and employment as shown in Figure 30.

The expected rate of profit
In the above numerical example shown in the boxed item, it is the firm's

expectations of the real rate of interest that determines whether the investment is undertaken. Expectations are the crucial thing in this case. As we saw, household expenditure can be very significantly affected by changes in the rate of interest on a mortgage. Firms are aware of this and will expect a lower level of demand from households as interest rates rise, and so expect lower sales and profits.

If firms become highly pessimistic about future profitability and growth they will be unwilling to invest – even at lower rates of interest – and so the investment demand curve will shift. This is shown on Figure 33, where the rise in interest rate causes firms to reduce their planned investment from I_1 to I_3. The fall from I_1 to I_2 is due to a movement along the investment demand curve ID_1 as before. The fall in investment from I_2 to I_3 is due to reduced business confidence. Firms know that other sectors of the economy will be affected by the rise in interest rates, leading to an overall fall in demand for goods and services, and they decide to invest less at all rates of interest.

The combined effect reduces aggregate demand significantly. This is exactly what the policymakers want in their anti-inflationary drive, but for some firms it will mean closure or cuts in output and employment. Firms that supply investment goods, vehicles or those in construction typically find they are worst hit as expansion plans are curtailed and machines are not replaced.

It should also be noted that the long-run effect of this fall in investment may be to reduce the rate of growth of the economy. The capacity output of the economy will consequently be less in future years – long-run aggregate supply will not move as far to the right – and there will be a lower level of real output.

The exchange rate

The exchange rate is also affected by interest rate changes. When the rate of interest in the UK rises relative to the rate of interest elsewhere, funds are attracted by the better return on sterling assets and there is consequently a higher demand for pounds. This causes the exchange rate to rise.

When the exchange rate rises, exports become more expensive in terms of foreign currencies and imports become cheaper in the UK. This loss of **competitiveness** could lead to lower sales of UK-produced goods and services, and so lower output and employment. UK firms therefore favour a lower rather than higher exchange rate, and so prefer to see UK interest rates relatively lower than those in other countries.

Summing up
From all of the above discussion we can conclude that industry and trade unions will always argue for lower interest rates. This brings them directly into opposition with the Bank of England when it raises interest rates in order to keep inflation in line with the government's inflation target.

Overall the effect of raising interest rates can be seen to have widespread consequences within the economy. The Bank of England must consider these wider effects when setting interest rates – indeed the MPC relies on them. It is by affecting the behaviour of households, firms and the exchange rate that monetary policy has an effect on the economy. Often these consequences can be severe and unpopular, because unemployment usually represents a personal tragedy for families, not just an 'economic cost'.

KEY WORDS

Savings
Mortgage repayments
Discretionary income
Houshold assets

Expected real rate of interest
Expected rate of profit
Competitiveness

Further reading
Davies, B., Hale, G., Smith, C. and Tiller, H., Chapter 4.25 in *Investigating Economics*, Macmillan, 1996.
Grant, S., Chapter 60 in *Stanlake's Introductory Economics*, Longman, 1999.
Howells, P. and Bain, K., Chapters 3, 4, 8 and 22 in *The Economics of Money, Banking and Finance: A European Text*, Addison-Wesley Longman, 1998.
Hutton, W., Chapter 3 in *The State We're In*, Jonathan Cape, 1995.

Useful website
CBI: www.cbi.org.uk

Essay questions
1. (a) Why might a country wish to restrain inflationary pressures? [40 marks]

(b) Examine the policies which a member country of the European Union might use in an attempt to prevent an increase in the domestic rate of inflation. [60 marks] [University of London Examinations and Assessment Council 1997]
2. (a) Explain the main features of monetary policy. [10 marks]
(b) Analyse the effects of an increase in interest rates on output, the price level and employment. [15 marks]

Data response question

This task is based on a question set by the University of Oxford Delegacy of Local Examinations in 1995. Read the following piece and study Table A. Then answer the questions that follow, using also your own knowledge of economic analysis and economic institutions.

Economic commentators don't normally agree about anything, but in one area they are unanimous: British housing policy is in a mess. Not only is it in a mess, it is having quite severe social effects and, because of its links with interest rates, the PSBR, and cost-push inflation, it plays a major undercover role in macroeconomic policy.

The root cause lies in the drive for owner-occupation. This has provided subsidies for house purchase in the form of tax relief on mortgage interest and the exemption of private house sales from capital gains tax. The subsidies have had the effect of boosting demand and raising house prices, but have also created a need for large mortgages with heavy interest payments attached to them. In the past these were accommodated by rapid inflation: this had the effect of raising wages and reducing the real value of mortgages, whilst boosting house prices and the scope for future tax-free capital gains. Nowadays, with low inflation, this escape route is closed.

Thus, there are now three groups in the private house market. Firstly, older homeowners who have paid off their mortgages, have savings that earn interest, want low inflation because of their fixed pensions, and are looking for capital gains. The second group is the opposite. These homeowners bought in the 1980s, at the peak of the housing boom. They now desperately need low interest rates to cut mortgage costs, and inflation to boost their wages and take them out of the negative equity trap and into potential capital gains.

Finally, there are the young who can't afford to be owner-occupiers and are faced with the ever-escalating costs of rented property. However, with the removal of rent ceilings and the drive for market rents, an increasing proportion find they cannot afford to pay such rents and end up on the streets. Alternatively, they fall back on government resources and add to the rising bill for housing benefit, thus increasing the PSBR. Thus, whilst the government has saved public expenditure on the one hand, by pushing the sale of council houses and limiting their new construction, it has increased it on the other hand.

Yes, British housing policy is in a mess.

Table A Data for the UK, 1985–93

	Average house prices (£000)	Annual % change			Unemployment (%)	Interest rate (%)
		Retail prices	Wages	GDP		
1985	31.1	6.0	8.5	3.8	10.9	12.0
1986	36.3	3.4	7.9	4.3	11.2	10.6
1987	40.4	4.2	7.8	4.8	10.2	9.4
1988	49.4	4.9	8.7	5.0	8.0	10.2
1989	54.8	7.8	9.2	2.2	6.3	13.8
1990	59.8	9.5	9.6	0.4	5.8	14.6
1991	62.5	5.9	8.0	-2.0	8.1	11.1
1992	60.8	3.7	6.1	-0.5	9.8	9.0
1993	62.7	1.6	3.4	2.0	10.3	5.2

Source: *Economic Trends* and *Social Trends*, Central Statistical Office, HMSO.

1. (a) What factors may affect the demand for houses for owner-occupation? [3 marks]
   (b) To what extent do the numerical data in the table give any indication as to which are the more important factors? [5 marks]
2. (a) Use supply and demand analysis to explain the argument about the effects of subsidies. [3 marks]
   (b) Under what conditions would the stated results not occur? [4 marks]
3. What links may exist between increases in house prices and consumers' expenditure? [10 marks]
4. Use the passage, data, and your own knowledge to evaluate the argument that a policy to achieve low inflation produces benefits to participants in the housing market. [15 marks]

Chapter Ten
European economic and monetary union

'*The risks to the economy of entering EMU without proper convergence are simply too great and hugely outweigh the economic benefits – which are modest.*'
Ruth Lea, Head of the Policy Unit, Institute of Directors, *EMU Briefing Paper*, March 1998

In this chapter we shall be concerned with what **economic and monetary union** (EMU) means for the implementation of monetary policy. Whether or not the UK should join EMU is largely beyond the scope of this book but is crucial to the future conduct of monetary policy. We shall examine what a single currency for Europe means, and how inflation is measured in the '**euro area**' (this is not an official term, but is useful shorthand). We finish with a brief look at the costs and benefits of the UK losing the ability to pursue an independent monetary policy.

What the single currency means

National currencies cease to exist
All existing currencies in the 'euro area' – those countries joining monetary union – will cease to exist. They will continue to circulate until the year 2002, but they are already locked together so their relative values will not change. In July 2002, French francs will no longer be accepted in shops in France; deutschemarks, marrka and lire will go the same way. Only the euro will be acceptable in settlement of debt.

A single inflation rate and interest rate
A single 'euro area' inflation rate will be calculated and a single interest rate set for the area.

A European central bank
One currency requires one central bank. Decisions on interest rates and the issuing of the currency passed to the **European Central Bank** (ECB) on 1 January 1999.

Table 5 The conversion exchange rates for the euro

Euro exchange rates: one euro is worth:	
Deutschemark	1.95583
French franc	6.55957
Italian lira	1936.21
Spanish peseta	166.386
Portugese escudo	200.482
Finnish markka	5.94573
Irish punt	0.787564
Dutch guilder	2.20371
Austrian schilling	13.7603
Belgian franc	40.3399
Luxembourg franc	40.3399

The rates against the £ and $ float:		
Sterling	0.704	On 31 December 1998
US dollar	1.169	On 31 December 1998

Exchange rates locked together
The first stage of the process saw the exchange rates of the 11 countries joining the 'first wave' permanently locked together at rates agreed on 31 December 1998. They are shown in Table 5. These rates mean that the euro already exists in all but physical form.

Monetary policy in the 'euro area'

Monetary policy in the 'euro area' is in the hands of the European Central Bank based in Frankfurt, Germany. A single currency requires a single central bank. The ECB has responsibility for providing and managing the euro and will take decisions on the level of interest rates.

The ECB has been established as an independent central bank. It is free from political control – only the members of the board of the ECB can make decisions on interest rates in order to meet their target of price stability.

The designers of the constitution of the ECB have tried to make it very obviously independent. This is partly because of the model established by the German Bundesbank which was very successful in pursuing its objective of price stability, free from political control. As the ECB does not have the track record of the Bundesbank to convince the markets of its anti-inflation credibility, the ECB has been made even more independent.

The ECB is at the centre of the **European System of Central Banks**

(ESCB), the central banks of the member nations, each of which is also required to be independent of their government. The Governing Council of the ECB will comprise the national central bank governors of the participating countries. Each member of the Council will have one vote, with the ECB President and Vice-President also voting.

The decisions on interest rates are made by the Governing Council with the implementation of policy delegated to the national central banks.

The Maastricht Treaty has given the ECB and ESCB one principal goal:

> '... the primary objective of the ESCB shall be to maintain price stabilty'.

The ECB can consider other objectives, but the Treaty is clear:

> 'Without prejudice to the objective of price stability, it shall support the general economic policies in the Community.' (Article 2)

In addition the ECB may not lend to national governments, or to EU organizations. Thus it cannot bail out profligate policies, nor fund inflationary expenditure programmes. The ECB can influence exchange rate policy, but has no other functions. It is concerned only with the management of the value of the euro.

The inflation target adopted by the ECB is 2 per cent on the **Monetary Union Index of Consumer Prices** (MUICP) for the 11 euro members. This is similar to the Bank of England's target of 2.5 per cent on the RPIX.

In essence the ECB has been set up in a way that is similar to the way the MPC operates in the UK. The design of the MPC may indeed have been deliberately similar to allow easier transition should the UK decide to join EMU at a later date.

Measuring inflation in the 'euro area'

It is necessary to have a measure of inflation for the 'euro area' that reflects the changing purchasing power of the currency. In the UK this is done by the retail price index (RPI); in the 'euro area' it is the monetary union index of consumer prices (MUICP), which is referred to as the **'harmonized rate'**.

The MUICP is based on indexes collected in the member states that are based on similar baskets of goods. The harmonized indexes use a basket of goods that is typical of the average spending of an EU household. This is different from any one national basket, but allows comparison across countries and the construction of an aggregate measure over all the EU countries.

The MUICP is made up of the weighted average of the 'harmonized index of consumer prices' (HICP) for the 11 'euro area' countries. The weight for each country is based on the country's share of private final domestic expenditure in the EMU total. The weights given to each country's index in 1998 are shown in Table 6: it is clear that price movements in Germany will have a great influence on the MUICP.

To see how the MUICP differs from the RPI, we can compare the weights assigned to various groups of goods in the RPI and the HICP for the UK in 1998 (see Table 7).

Table 7 shows clearly that the harmonized index gives less weight to housing expenses. This is largely explained by the lower incidence of owner-occupation in the EU as a whole than in the UK, and the fact that in the UK fixed-rate mortgages are unusual, but are common in the rest of Europe. The treatment of insurance is also very different between the two, but this is not obvious from the table.

It should be clear from the above that the two indexes will give different inflation figures for the UK. In December 1998 the RPI gave a figure of 3 per cent, the RPIX 2.5 per cent, and the HICP 1.4 per cent.

The difference between the RPIX and HICP figures can be accounted for. About 0.5 percentage points of the difference are due to the way the index is calculated – the RPIX uses arithmetic means,

Table 6 The weights given to domestic price indexes in MUICP

Country	Weight
Belgium	38.0
Germany	345.2
Spain	89.0
France	218.7
Ireland	9.0
Italy	181.7
Luxembourg	2.2
Netherlands	53.5
Austria	30.4
Portugal	16.8
Finland	15.5
EMU (total)	1000.0

Source: Eurostat.

Table 7 The UK's RPI and HICP compared

Goods group	RPI weight	UK HICP weight
Food and non alcoholic beverages	130	156
Alcohol and tobacco	105	70
Clothing and footwear	55	67
Housing and fuel	233	134
Household furnishings and services	108	90
Transport	156	154
Recreation and culture	117	131
Hotels and restaurants	48	111
Communications	18	21
Miscellaneous	30	66
Totals	1000	1000

the HICP uses geometric means. The remaining 2 percentage point difference from the HICP must be due to the construction of the basket of goods.

Implications for UK economic policy of joining EMU

There are two principal implications for domestic economic policy if the UK joins EMU and adopts the euro in place of the pound:

- domestic monetary policy will cease to be available, and
- fiscal policy will be constrained by the stability pact.

- Monetary policy under EMU

The ECB sets interests rates for the 'euro area', and so if the UK adopts the euro the Bank of England will cease to be responsible for monetary policy in the UK. No matter how much the UK government wanted interest rates in the UK to be different from those in the rest of Europe, it would be powerless to change them.

- Fiscal policy under EMU

Under a **growth and stability pact** agreed in 1997, no member of the 'euro area' may run a budget deficit in the medium term. As a practical measure, 3 per cent of GDP is seen as the maximum borrowing requirement any country could allow.

The implications of this are that member governments of the 'euro area' must give up considerable freedom in policy instruments to gain the advantages of the single currency.

Should the UK join EMU?

This is a matter of considerable and ongoing debate. It is not possible to do justice to the arguments here, nor is that the purpose of the book. The loss of UK monetary policy would, however, change over half of the subject matter of this book and so we shall briefly examine the cases for and against.

The crucial issue can be thought of as a cost–benefit analysis. The benefits of EMU are the advantages of having a single currency over a wider area – Europe. The costs are the loss of an adjustable exchange rate and loss of domestic policy freedom. The boxed item lists the costs and benefits without assigning weight to any point.

FUNDAMENTAL COSTS AND BENEFITS OF JOINING EMU

Costs of losing the £
- The exchange rate is lost as a 'shock absorber' for the economy
- Loss of control of monetary policy
- Fiscal policy restricted by *growth and stability pact.*

Benefits of joining EMU
- Transactions costs are eliminated in trade within 'euro area'
- Exchange rate uncertainty is eliminated within 'euro area'
- Monetary policy is handed to an independent central bank

- **The costs of joining**

The costs can be seen as being dramatic *if the UK economy seriously diverges from the rest of the euro area.* Suppose that there is a 'shock' to the economic system that affects the UK differently from other European nations, and this shock leads to a fall in demand for UK goods, while it causes a rise in demand for German goods.

If the pound exists then this shock can be cushioned by a devaluation of the pound against the German currency, now the euro. UK goods will become relatively cheaper and German goods relatively more expensive, and so the loss of output and employment in the UK will be less than if both countries have the same currency. If the UK were to join the euro, devaluation would not be an option.

The UK government could help to reduce the impact of the shock on UK business by raising its spending, or reducing taxation. This would, other things being equal, raise the government budget deficit; but this is limited by the aforementioned growth and stability pact.

Finally, the UK government could help to offset the shock by altering the rate of interest downwards in order to reduce firms' costs, while raising investment and consumer spending. This option would not be available if the UK joins the 'euro area'.

- **The benefits of joining**

When firms trade in another country with a different currency there must be a transaction on the foreign exchange market, and for this the traders take a commission. For trade within the 'euro area' this foreign exchange market transaction is not needed, and so the commission charged is eliminated, a direct cost saving to those engaged in trade.

Exchange rates cannot be guaranteed even a few months into the future. When firms trade across national boundaries they usually need to set prices far in advance, and if the exchange rate moves in the meantime they can find themselves making a loss or charging more than they need to, so losing sales. A single currency eliminates this risk and so encourages lower prices and more trade.

The independent central bank, the ECB, being free from political control, is unlikely to engage in vote-catching reflations. As its only aim is price stability this should mean that the 'euro area' can be more confident of the ECB achieving its aim, and price stability is good for firms' confidence and so investment.

- **Krugman's analysis**

The economist Paul Krugman has shown how the costs and benefits so expressed fall and rise respectively with the **degree of integration** between the economies concerned. Figure 34 expresses costs and benefits as a percentage of GDP (vertical axis) and integration as the ratio of inter-union trade to GDP.

The costs curve shows that the cost of EMU would decline as integration increases, while the benefit rises with integration. If this analysis is correct, as the EU becomes more integrated then at some time the degree of integration t^* will be passed and the benefit of EMU will outweigh the cost. Some EU economies may have already passed t^*, others may not have.

There seems some reason to suppose, however, that the UK is not a typical EU economy and has yet to reach the point t^*. For example, interest rate changes affect the UK economy quite differently from the rest of Europe. One reason for this is that borrowers and lenders in the UK have a much higher proportion of loans with variable interest rates. In Europe most loans have fixed rates of interest. Thus a change in interest rates in the UK has a far greater impact on UK residents than it

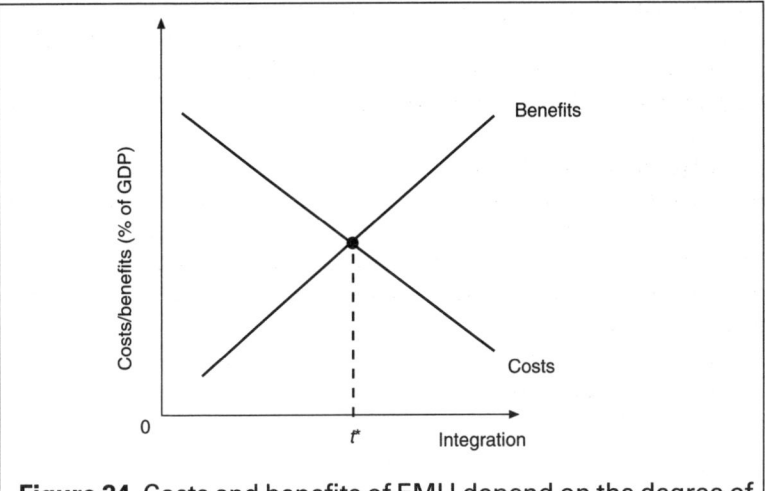

Figure 34 Costs and benefits of EMU depend on the degree of integration

does on European citizens (this is discussed in Chapter 9).

The UK also follows a different economic cycle from the rest of Europe. This can mean that when the UK is in recession, and needs lower interest rates, the rest of Europe is facing inflation and needs higher ones. Convergence of economic cycles would seem to be required for successful entry into EMU.

The UK has wider-ranging world trade interests than other 'euro area' countries, who traditionally trade much more with each other. Therefore the potential benefits of EMU for the UK are not as great as for other European countries.

Krugman's analysis is limited in its approach, but does provide a useful framework. While it is not sufficient simply to meet Krugman's point t^* for successful monetary union, it could be argued it is necessary to meet it.

KEY WORDS

European monetary union
'Euro area'
European Central Bank
European System of Central Banks

Monetary Union Index of Consumer Prices
Harmonized rate
Growth and stability pact
Degree of integration

Further reading
Artis, M.J. and Lee, N., Chapter 13 in *The Economics of the European Union*, 2nd edn, Oxford University Press, 1997.

Cook, G., *The Single European Currency: A Student's Guide*, Hidcote Press, 1998.

El-Agraa, A., Chapter 5 in *The European Union*, 5th edn, Prentice Hall, 1998.

Healy, N., Chapter 3 in *European Economic Integration*, 3rd edn (eds F. McDonald and S. Dearden), Addison-Wesley Longman, 1999.

Useful websites
One in favour and one against.
Association for Monetary Union (*for*): www.amue.lf.net/
Business for Sterling (*against*): www.bfors.com

Essay topics
1. (a) Discuss the role of the European Central Bank. [10 marks]
   (b) Explain why a rise in the 'euro area' interest rate may have a more beneficial effect on the economies of some member countries than others. [15 marks]
2. To what extent may individual countries that are members of the European monetary union have control over their macroeconomy? [40 marks] [University of Oxford Delegacy of Local Examinations 1999]

Data response question
Read the following extract from an article by Larry Elliot that appeared in the *Guardian* on 7 June 1999. Then answer the questions that follow, using also your own knowledge of economic analysis.

Given what has happened since 1 January, it is difficult to claim that the euro is a stable and strong currency, so the case now is that Britain is too small and weak to go it alone.

Let's look at this argument in detail. Britain is not a small and weak economy. It has overtaken an Italy hobbled by the preparations for monetary union and – along with France – has the fourth largest gross domestic product of any nation.

A second argument is that you cannot have a single market without a single currency, something that the rest of Europe has recognised, but not Britain.

But according to the devotees of the euro, Britain does not have an independent monetary policy anyway but could free itself from German thraldom if it joined the single currency.

The European central bank is a way that the rest of Europe can take back some control of interest rates from the Bundesbank rather than meekly accepting whatever Germany deems necessary.

This is the strangest argument of the lot. The reason that euroland's interest rate is 2.5% is because that is what is good for Germany, not what is good for Ireland, Portugal or Spain. In addition, it is quite untrue that Britain is incapable of running its own monetary policy, because this is precisely what it has been doing with considerable success since 16 September 1992.

Unshackled from the exchange rate mechanism, recovery from recession began almost immediately and has been embedded by a macroeconomic policy regime which, if not perfect, is certainly far superior to that in euroland.

The use of a symmetrical inflation target, the better co-ordination of monetary and fiscal policy, the greater transparency and accountability of decision making, are real strengths that countries in the single currency zone lack.

Supporters of the single currency believe that a sceptical public can be bought by the promise of lower interest rates and not having to change their pounds into pesetas on the Costa Blanca. So far, voters seem resistant.

1. Why might a single currency make a single market work more effectively? [4 marks]
2. Discuss the extent to which Britain currently has an independent monetary policy. [6 marks]
3. Explain what is meant by (i) the exchange rate mechanism, and (ii) a symmetrical inflation target. [2 + 2 marks]
4. Identify and explain *three* advantages of joining the single currency which are mentioned in the extract. [6 marks]
5. What advantages my Britain gain from delaying its entry into EMU? [5 marks]

Conclusion

Since 1971, when the fixed exchange-rate system (the Bretton Woods system) set up after the Second World War broke down, the world monetary system has lacked stability. Indeed the history of inflation and monetary policy has been almost chaotic. Exchange rates have floated freely and money has been linked to nothing at all. Not surprisingly, the supply of money expanded rapidly.

The conflicting views on inflation we examined in Chapter 4 can perhaps be put into a longer term context. The cause of rising prices in the short term may be due to any of the possibilities discussed; but a persistent rise in the money supply over nearly 30 years, which is not offset by a rise in real output, is bound to see a rise in the price level as predicted by the monetarists. The problem of running monetary policy in this period has been compounded by rapid institutional and technological changes both within the UK and internationally. It is no surprise, therefore, to see nations seek a new monetary standard such as the ERM or the single European currency.

At present the rate of inflation in the UK is not the acute problem it used to be. This is partly due to a period of prolonged recession in the early 1990s and the now rapidly falling prices of some commodities as a result of new technologies and globalization. Unusually as the century closes, deflation is a concern for the first time in over 50 years, if only a slight one.

The UK has now embarked on a new framework for monetary policy. The monetary policy committee (MPC) has instrumental independence to achieve its assigned target. At the same time the UK must coexist with a new major currency, the euro, or in due course join it and abandon independent monetary policy. As usual there is great uncertainty over the future course of events.

Of the MPC we can say: 'so far, so good'. Inflation appears to be under control and on target. The MPC has been actively pursuing a vigorous policy, against the majority of expectations that it would demonstrate a conservative approach that emphasized safety. The euro has had a difficult start to life, but at the time of writing there can be no firm conclusions drawn – except perhaps that 'ownership' of the euro is confused, with national finance ministers and the European Central Bank making conflicting statements about its current status.

Index

Anticipated inflation 22
Asset prices 105

Bank of England 61–2, 86, 90, 91–2
Base rate 69
Base year 14
Bonds 66, 70

Central bank
  functions 60–2
  independence 86, 94–5
Consumption 107–8
Cost-push inflation 40–3, 57–8
Credit controls 78
Credit creation 63–4
Credit multiplier 64

Deflation 4, 28
Degrees of inflation 8
Demand for money 68–9
Demand-pull inflation 34–9, 57–8
Deregulation 56
Disintermediation 79
Domestically generated inflation 43–5

Euro area 112
European central bank (ECB) 112–14
European monetary union (EMU) 112–20
European system of central banks (ESCB) 113–14
Exchange rate mechanism (ERM) 77, 82–3
Exchange rates 25, 41–2, 70–1, 76–7, 81–3, 108–9, 113

Expectations augmented Phillips curve 49–52

Family expenditure survey (FES) 10–11
Fan chart 90–3
Financial markets 60–1
Fiscal drag/boost 26
Fiscal policy 60, 80–1
Fisher equation 33
Fixed exchange rates 76–7
Functions of money 63
Funding 81

GDP deflator 19
Government securities – see bonds
Growth and stability pact 116

Harmonized index of consumer prices (HICP) 19, 114–6
Headline inflation (RPI) 17
Hyper-inflation 8

Imported inflation 41–5
Indexation 27
Inflation
  alternative measures 17–9
  defined 3, 6
  pure 7
  rate 8
  targeting 17, 83, 86–8, 98
Inflation Report 84–8, 91, 94
Inflationary gap 36
Interest rates
  as policy tool 68–72, 80–1, 91–2
  effect on economy 70–2, 91–2, 101–9
  movements in UK 80
International competitiveness 25

Investment 106–8

Keynesians 36–40, 48
Keynesian monetary policy 76–8
Krugman's analysis 118–19

Labour productivity 40
Labour markets 41–2
Liquidity 64, 70
Long-run Phillips curve 50–2
Long-run supply 33

Medium term financial strategy (MTFS) 79–81
Menu costs 22
Monetarists 31–6, 48–52
Monetary accommodation/validation 46
Monetary base control 67–8
Monetary policy
 aims 64, 86
 defined 60
 implementation pre 1997 76–84
 implementation post 1997 86–93
 techniques 65–72
 under EMU 116–17
Monetary policy committee (MPC) 86–98
Money supply
 and the price level 53–6
 defined 62–3
 M0, M4 53, 55–6, 62–3
Mortgages 103–4

NAIRU 52
Natural rate of output 33
Natural rate of un/employment 50–2

Nominal values 7

Open market operations 66
Output gap 28

Phillips curve 39–40, 48–52, 77
Policy instruments and targets 72
Political business cycle 94
Price mechanism 4–6
Prices and incomes policy 77–8
Purchasing power 6–7

Quantity theory of money 32–4, 52–6

Real wages 48
Real values 7
Redistribution effects 24–5
Repo rate 92
Retail price index 10–17

Saving 102–3
Shoe-leather costs 22
Special deposits 67
Stagflation 48

Time lags 72–3
Transmission mechanism 65–6

Unanticipated inflation 22
Uncertainty 24
Underlying inflation (RPIX, RPIY) 17

Velocity of circulation 32, 55–6

Wage differentials 45
Wage-price spiral 45, 57
Weights (in index numbers) 11